# VIETNAMESE CUISINE IN NEW ORLEANS

# VIETNAMESE CUISINE

## in New Orleans

By Suzanne Pfefferle

Photographs by Lenny Delbert, Sr.,
and Suzanne Pfefferle

**PELICAN PUBLISHING COMPANY**

Gretna 2014

*The word "Pelican" and the depiction of a pelican are
trademarks of Pelican Publishing Company, Inc., and are
registered in the U.S. Patent and Trademark Office.*

ISBN 9781455618538
E-book ISBN 9781455618545

Printed in China

Published by Pelican Publishing Company, Inc.
1000 Burmaster Street, Gretna, Louisiana 70053

*To Dorothy "Dottie" Hubert Jumonville (1919-2009), a spirited lady who spoke her mind and doled out love like there was no tomorrow,*

*and*

*Donald Burvant Pfefferle (1925-2012), a "Little Pepper" who dreamed big and lived each day with purpose and passion*

# Contents

# VIETNAMESE CUISINE IN NEW ORLEANS

# Introduction

My foray into Vietnamese food began in November of 2010. A dear friend of mine was leaving New Zealand and traveling throughout Southeast Asia, en route to the United States. Another friend, whom I have known since preschool, had just completed a teaching stint in Hanoi. And I was about to earn my two-week vacation from work.

An avid traveler, I had already ticked Egypt, Jamaica, and India off of my list. I had a keen interest in the history of Vietnam, which involved devastating conflicts set in a tropical paradise. I wanted to learn about the culture and countryside, firsthand. So when it came to choosing a place for us to convene, Vietnam was the top pick. I have taken trips abroad since then and can say that my journey to Vietnam was the most humbling, humorous, exhilarating—oh, and *delicious*— of them all.

My flight to Vietnam, which included stops in Los Angeles and Seoul, South Korea, was more than thirty hours. And I lack the ability to snooze soundly during lengthy flights. So when I landed in Saigon at midnight (my friends had arrived the day before me), I hailed a cab, headed straight for my hotel, and climbed into bed.

I woke up feeling groggy but brimming with eagerness to explore the city (nice try, jetlag). Although I was craving a decadent pastry or something greasy, my friends suggested a bowl of *phở gà*, which I initially thought was similar to chicken noodle soup. This seemed like an odd choice for breakfast, but I went with it.

To my surprise, *phở* kitchens were teeming with locals at that hour. Street vendors, nestled in narrow alleyways shaded by clusters of clotheslines, scooped aromatic broth into bowls and served them to sleepy customers. When I looked around, I did not spot a single person eating an omelet or munching on crispy cereal.

It seemed that everyone was mindlessly lifting chopsticks to their lips, slurping long rice noodles, and savoring the flavorful *phở* broth. After my first bowl, I understood why. The combination of carbohydrates, protein from meat, zesty herbs, and rich, but not heavy, broth gave me the energy to take on the day. Good morning, Vietnam!

In Saigon, popup stands offering *bánh mì* proved to be abundant. At small cafes, lines of chattering customers snaked around the counter and out of the door. I watched with fascination as one cook briskly swiped ecru-colored mayonnaise onto baguette bread, layered one piece of charcuterie over another, tucked the substantial-size sandwich into a sleeve of wax paper, and handed it to the cashier—all without lifting her eyes. The finished product, bursting with an assortment of flavors, set me back a mere two dollars.

While I was sitting on the bus en route to the city of Da Lat, I pulled my *bánh mì* out of my backpack and unwrapped the wax paper, unsure of what to expect. *It was love at first bite!* It was unlike anything I had ever eaten. From sweet and spicy, to crunchy and soft, a mix of flavors and textures danced on my palate.

Then I chomped into a slice of juicy jalapeño pepper. Sweat trickled down the side of my flushed face as I took a swig of water and swished it around my mouth. Though I finished my sandwich with watery eyes, I enjoyed every bite. That was my first of many *bánh mì* experiences. But now I tend to keep my eyes peeled for hot jalapeño peppers.

Although I began each day of my Far East excursion with a bowl of *phở*, along with a *cà phê sữa đá,* an eye-opening, caffeinated concoction, I explored other areas of authentic Vietnamese cuisine. Taking tips from locals was key.

Though the bustling city of Saigon boasted five-star restaurants, sidewalk bistros, and hip eateries full of college students, a handful of street vendors, serving home-cooked meals, could be found on every block. Since we were budget travelers searching for a taste of pure Vietnamese food, we frequented these stalls with pleasure. We often found ourselves passing around plates of exotic food and sipping icy Tiger® beers while chatting in choppy Vietnamese with locals.

We would watch the vibrant nightlife of Saigon unfold before our eyes. Motorcycles zipped down the street, owners of souvenir shops beckoned to oblivious pedestrians, and locals danced in alfresco nightclubs. After indulging in a typical dinner of barbecue pork or steamed clams covered in slivers of lemongrass, my comrades and I would munch on fresh chunks of dragon fruit and sweet rice, coated in coconut shavings, for dessert.

While in Mui Ne, a sleepy beach town in South Vietnam, we sampled a myriad of seafood delights. The main avenue was peppered with street-food vendors preparing meals over open flames. The options for a maritime feast seemed endless.

We indulged in fresh squid, jumbo shrimp kebabs stacked atop juicy wedges of pineapple, catfish that had been caramelized in a clay pot, types of crab I had never seen before, and tender shark, covered in a sweet sauce. As a New Orleanian who loves seafood, I was in heaven.

*Bánh xèo is a Vietnamese crepe topped with slivers of meat and herbs.* (Photograph by Suzanne Pfefferle)

Despite the assortment of food items I discovered during my travels, I found myself opting for small, already-assembled meals that I could toss into my backpack and save for later. The *bánh mì* sandwich quickly became a favorite. But then I discovered *bánh bao*. These fluffy, steamed, wheat-flour dumplings contain a center of seasoned meat—usually pork or chicken—and small vegetables, such as green peas and shredded carrot. Sometimes, half of a hardboiled egg is tucked into the mix. It is often tinted green by a banana leaf. Biting into the center and discovering the hidden flavor was like embarking on a small treasure hunt—or selecting a truffle from a box of chocolates. What would I find? I was always surprised but never let down.

The beverages that we sampled in Vietnam complemented the hot and often humid climate. Beer—from Tiger® to Singha®—was served in a glass mug, with a thick chunk of ice floating in the middle. On the rare occasion that we ordered a bottle of red wine, it was brought to the table in a bucket of ice.

*While I was in Mui Ne, this lovely Vietnamese lady introduced me to* bánh xèo. *(Photograph by Suzanne Pfefferle)*

But the most popular beverage available was *cà phê sữa đá*. This jolting drink features strong coffee, slowly dripped over a glass of ice, and often contains a generous layer of dulcet condensed milk, which is whisked into the mixture with a spoon.

*I began each day of my trip with an energizing* cà phê sữa đá.
(Photograph by Suzanne Pfefferle)

*The countryside is peppered with coffee plantations, releasing a rich aroma of freshly roasted beans.* (Photograph by Suzanne Pfefferle)

During our final week in Vietnam, one friend and I took a thorough walking tour throughout the streets of Saigon. I was surprised to discover that there was a bakery on nearly every block. One in particular boasted a sign in French script and outdoor bistro tables, nestled under brightly colored umbrellas. My friend and I popped in for an afternoon snack and espresso. Judging by the crowd, it seemed like the place to be.

Taking a cue from other customers, we each picked up a tray from a stand situated at the entrance. Rather than selecting a pastry from behind a glass-covered counter, we waltzed around the room acquiring an assortment of pastries, which were neatly stacked on buffet tables. We sat down and shared our loot, which between the both of us included bear claws, flaky croissants, a couple of cookies, oddly shaped pastries that I had never seen before, two Napoleons, and a warm cinnamon bun that was as big as my head.

While sipping on strong espressos, we devoured our delicacies, too enthralled by the deliciousness to bother with conversation. This unexpected French twist concluded our culinary expedition through Vietnam.

Though our visit to Vietnam seemed to revolve around copious amounts of food, we set aside an ample amount of time to learn about the history of the country—particularly the Vietnam War. We stopped by an art gallery in Saigon that displayed propaganda posters from the 1970s and toured the Cu Chi Tunnels, an elaborate network of underground passages that the Vietnamese used to evade the opposition.

Then we visited the much-talked-about War Remnants Museum. Learning about the atrocities of this horrific war—from a new perspective—was the most shocking and sobering moment of my stay in Vietnam.

War relics, along with a photographic timeline, led guests to the Fall of Saigon, which took place in 1975 when the Communist North

Vietnamese gained control of the South. During the chaos, tens of thousands of Vietnamese began fleeing the country, leaving their belongings behind, and headed into the unknown. Many found themselves in the United States—and, eventually, in New Orleans.

When I arrived back in New Orleans, I felt compelled to learn more about the Vietnamese, beyond their wonderful cuisine. I ventured out to New Orleans East, where there is a thriving Vietnamese community—Village de l'Est. I learned about their advanced urban agriculture practices; weekly outdoor famers' markets, reminiscent of those in Vietnam; family traditions; and community celebrations, such as the lively *Têt* festival, the Vietnamese New Year. The community celebrates this event the same way they embrace life—with gusto, optimism, and faith. They are true New Orleanians.

I am not a food writer. I am an advocate for cultural preservation and admire the Vietnamese for celebrating their heritage and sharing it with others in the New Orleans community. I have produced a film about the Vietnamese community and their cuisine and have now written a book, but I believe that I have only completed the first chapter.

During my research, I met inspiring individuals in this community. I so look forward to developing future collaborations and new friendships with local Vietnamese Americans. Who would have thought that all of this would stem from a vacation with my long-time friends? It is proof that traveling takes me places, indeed. Enjoy the journey.

Chapter 1

# New Orleans Embraces Vietnamese Cuisine

Fans of Vietnamese cuisine from New Orleans once traveled to New Orleans East or the West Bank for a taste of this exotic fare. While restaurants such as Ba Mien on Chef Menteur Highway and Tan Dinh on Lafayette Street still boast an impressive following, new Vietnamese eateries have sprouted in popular New Orleans neighborhoods.

"In the last few years, there's been this proliferation of Vietnamese restaurants across the city. But it has been taking root for a long time," says food writer Ian McNulty. McNulty recalls editing a restaurant guide for diners on a budget around 2004. His editors encouraged him to include "off the beaten track" eateries.

"Driving from the center of New Orleans to the West Bank was a major culinary safari," he jokes. But these commutes led to an awareness of Vietnamese restaurants. "Now, more people are making those treks. And they are seeing more restaurants popping up in different parts of town."

Magasin Café, with its sleek decor, sits on the corner of Magazine Street and Milan. This bustling restaurant features nine varieties of fresh summer rolls, *gỏi cuốn*, including lemongrass grilled chicken and garlic fried tofu. Magasin also offers contemporary twists on traditional Vietnamese-cuisine staples, such as *phở*, or rice-noodle soup. Owners Luu Tran and Kim Nguyen note that the *phở* filet mignon is a crowd favorite.

*A young girl enjoys a Vietnamese feast with her father at Magasin Café.* (Photograph by Lenny Delbert, Sr.)

Lilly's Café and Phở Noi Viet, in the Lower Garden District, attract young professionals from the Central Business District, college students, and neighborhood residents.

And while dipping fresh summer rolls into peanut sauce, diners at Le Viet Café on St. Charles Avenue can watch the streetcar rumble down its route. Owner Tiffany Le, whose family ran a restaurant in Vietnam, saw a need for a Vietnamese restaurant in the Uptown area. "My menu is small, because I want to keep it authentic," she says.

In Mid-City, the Eat Well market contains a small deli that offers authentic Vietnamese fare. Co-owner Triet Tra prepares beef *phở*,

*Beef* phở *(left) and summer rolls (right), with a peanut dipping sauce, from Le Viet Café* (Photograph by Lenny Delbert, Sr.)

barbecue pork *bánh mì*, and crab Rangoon. She also serves traditional New Orleans dishes, such as red beans and rice and po'-boy sandwiches.

Since opening the deli in early 2012, Tra has worked here with her husband and sons. Most of the patrons who frequent Eat Well are not familiar with Vietnamese fare but finish their meal pleasantly surprised.

Even non-Vietnamese restaurants, including August, Borgne, and Green Goddess, serve variations of the cuisine.

Chef Brian Landry, the executive chef of Borgne, prepares such

*Triet Tra co-owns the Eat Well market in Mid-City.* (Photograph by Lenny Delbert, Sr.)

*Tra prepares a beef-based Vietnamese dish.* (Photograph by Lenny Delbert, Sr.)

Asian-inspired delights as Fr. Vien's Chicken Salad. This dish, which was named after a former priest of Mary Queen of Vietnam, features a mixture of aromatic herbs and shredded chicken placed in bibb lettuce cups. Landry was introduced to the cuisine when he began cooking with Chef Dominique Macquet at Dominique's. "There was a gentleman named Quan Tran," he recalls. "He is of Vietnamese descent and lived out in New Orleans East. On our days off, he would take me out to New Orleans East, and we'd go eat at the Vietnamese restaurants and visit the farmers' market. One of the things I love about Vietnamese cuisine is that they do a great job of balancing flavors and textures. So you get a great mix of salty, sweet, sour, and spice. But you also get hot, cold, crunchy, and soft—typically in the same dish."

Paul Artigues of Green Goddess, located on a cobbled walkway in

*Brian Landry, executive chef of Borgne* (Photograph by Lenny Delbert, Sr.)

the French Quarter, offers a pork belly *bánh mì*. This bestseller features Cambodian-style pan-fried pork belly, Gulf shrimp coated in a Thai chili sauce, jalapeños, arugula, basil, pickled turnips, and fried shallots. A fresh baguette from Dong Phuong Bakery in New Orleans East encloses the flavorful ingredients.

Chef John Besh—owner of Restaurant August, Besh Steak, Domenica, Lüke New Orleans, Lüke San Antonio, La Provence, Soda Shop, the American Sector, and Borgne—remains one of the most well known advocates of Vietnamese cuisine and a staunch supporter

*Chef John Besh, owner of nine restaurants and advocate of the Vietnamese community* (Photograph by Lenny Delbert, Sr.)

of the local community. His connection to the cuisine began with a cooking job at the Windsor Court, where he worked with several Vietnamese ladies. "I was like the young, new guy. And they would feed me. Their maternal instincts took over," Besh reminisces. "I'd have these great soups and pan-fried noodle dishes."

Besh continues, "Years later, I'm employing some of their granddaughters and grandsons and working with the family." From baptisms to weddings, he began participating in their family celebrations. "It's very important for me to make sure that people don't forget that we have this Vietnamese component to the great city of New Orleans."

Because of his close interaction with the Vietnamese community, he's developed an affinity for creating classic New Orleans dishes with an Asian twist. Besh's shrimp Creole includes traces of garlic, ginger, cilantro, and chopped lemongrass, with a touch of chili paste, served over a heap of Louisiana jasmine rice.

But the popularity of the cuisine extends beyond the restaurant scene. At Jazz Fest and Po-Boy Fest, Vietnamese fare is available. At the Streetfare Derby, an annual gathering of local food trucks at the New Orleans Fair Grounds, Geaux Plates food truck offers its popular bayou *bánh mì*. The truck also serves this Vietnamese-inspired sandwich in various locations throughout the city on a regular basis.

"Bayou *bánh mì*, from day one, has been our bestseller," says owner Andrew Gomila. This treat features a seven-inch baguette from Dong Phuong Bakery cradling homemade boudin, lemongrass grilled chicken, cilantro, pickled carrots, chilies, and garlic-chili aioli. "It seems like an odd combination for someone who's never tried Vietnamese food," he admits. "But it works."

Because Vietnamese cuisine is appearing at crowded festivals and renowned restaurants and near various nightlife venues, New Orleanians have become aware of its significance and are more willing to give it a try. "It's going to become a mainstay part of the

*A couple enjoys the bayou* bánh mì *from Geaux Plates at the New Orleans Streetfare Derby.* (Photograph by Lenny Delbert, Sr.)

New Orleans culture," says Poppy Tooker, the producer and host of *Louisiana Eats!* on WWNO radio. "Now that it's right under our noses, the cuisine is going to become as common as Szechuan and Cantonese."

# Chapter 2

# Fresh and Healthy Fare

Vietnamese cuisine has become a local favorite for many reasons. But the strongest consensus among fans is that it is generally fresh and healthy. A single dish contains only a small portion of thinly sliced meat and achieves bold flavors through the use of zesty herbs, such as cilantro and basil, rather than rich sauces and oil. The foundation of these herb-laden dishes is *bánh phở,* flat rice noodles.

"Everything tastes like it was just plucked from the garden, thrown into the pot—and didn't spend much time in the pot at all—before it landed on your plate," says Poppy Tooker. The longer an ingredient is cooked, the less nutritional value it retains. "When it is so fresh, clean, and beautiful—and the flavors are dazzling—it's a real taste treat."

The emphasis on crisp ingredients stems from the cooking habits practiced in Vietnam. "In Vietnam, they don't have a freezer or walk-in cooler," says Chef Minh Bui of Café Minh. "Usually, the wife had to go to the market twice a day to buy vegetables and meat. So the food is always fresh."

In New Orleans—a city that embraces cuisines from numerous cultures—dishes with a high caloric content, such as fried food or a meal soaked in heavy sauces, remain abundant. Though New Orleanians celebrate timeless dishes such as crawfish étouffée, they find the lightness of Vietnamese food a pleasant change of pace.

*Poppy Tooker, the producer and host of* Louisiana Eats! *on WWNO radio, loves the freshness of Vietnamese cuisine.* (Photograph by Lenny Delbert, Sr.)

People have become increasingly scrupulous about the foods they consume and maintaining a healthier lifestyle, while looking for tasty new options in New Orleans' vast dining landscape. "With Vietnamese food, you can have something very flavorful but also kind of light," notes Chef John Besh. "And you feel good about it."

Former congressman Joseph Cao attributes the popularity of Vietnamese cuisine to its bonus of being nutritious. "For most of us who are conscientious about our health, there's an attraction towards the Vietnamese cuisine." As an example, he cites a standard Vietnamese chicken salad, which is prepared with lime juice, fish sauce, herbs, and peppers, rather than mayonnaise. "We usually season Vietnamese dishes with fish sauce, which is extremely light," he notes.

Fish sauce, *nước mắm,* is created by placing raw, salt-cured anchovies into a barrel, where they marinate. To make a dipping sauce, chefs and cooks combine *nước mắm* with other ingredients, such as sugar, vinegar, and lime juice.

Cilantro, an ingredient that is prevalent in Vietnamese cuisine, contains antibacterial compounds, dietary fiber, and magnesium. Another common trait of the cuisine is its use of red chili, which benefits the cardiovascular system.

*The fresh summer rolls from Le Viet Café consist of moist rice paper wrapped around meat or shellfish, vermicelli noodles, and herbs.* (Photograph by Lenny Delbert, Sr.)

One healthy menu item, which is probably the most popular, is *phở*, the rice-noodle soup. The national dish of Vietnam, *phở* is essentially a bowl of flavorful broth, anchored by long rice noodles, brimming with savory greens and topped with crunchy bean sprouts. Though *phở* appears in a myriad of forms, the most common variations are *phở bo*, which is made with beef broth, and chicken-broth-based *phở ga*.

Fresh summer rolls put the healthy traits of Vietnamese foods on prime display. Moist, translucent rice paper, or *bánh tráng*, envelops slivers of pork or prawns, savory greens, and rice vermicelli (*bún*). These appetizers, served at room temperature, allow the diner to see each fresh ingredient.

Even the fried foods on a Vietnamese menu contain less calories and fat than their counterparts in other Asian cuisines. A small wok, which requires less oil than a large Chinese wok, is used for frying. "When you eat at a traditional Cantonese restaurant, you roll out of there feeling like Buddha himself," says Tooker. "When you eat Vietnamese food, it energizes you. You're ready to go on and run an extra mile that day."

Since a Vietnamese meal traditionally involves several small dishes, blended at the table, the diner can control the portion size and customize the meal.

# Chapter 3

# Favorite Dishes

*Bánh bao*, or steamed buns, can be found at a variety of local Vietnamese restaurants. During a recent trip to Dong Phuong, I saw a petit baker carry a metal tray stacked with fresh *bánh bao* through the crowded bakery. Eager hands reached for the bundles until the tray was empty.

Le Viet Café also offers *bánh bao*. "That's like our snack," says owner Tiffany Le. And she claims that it is quite easy to prepare. "You pick what flavor you like, put it in the dough, and place it in the steamer."

Bánh bao *is a crowd favorite at Dong Phuong.* (Photograph by Lenny Delbert, Sr.)

*These brightly hued steamed buns are stuffed with savory fillings.* (Photograph by Lenny Delbert, Sr.)

*Roasted duck from Tan Dinh* (Photograph by Lenny Delbert, Sr.)

In terms of overlooked food items, New Orleans is abundant with options. The city is a mecca for adventurous eaters.

The owner of Tan Dinh recommends their udon soup with pork or their sticky rice with roasted duck. Another good choice is their short ribs with kimchee. Kimchee, which is pickled napa cabbage with spices and ginger, adds a burst of flavor to this exotic dish.

When Chef John Besh dines on Vietnamese cuisine with his family, he favors Ba Mien in New Orleans East. "They make these little rice-flour dumplings with pork," he says. Known as *bánh cuốn*, these cradle seasoned pork, minced wood-ear mushrooms, and shallots.

The dumpling is made by pouring rice batter onto a cloth that is stretched over a pot of boiling water. The batter is spread into a thin sheet, which, when steamed, is lifted by chopstick and placed onto a preparation table. It is then layered with vegetables and a type of meat and rolled into the shape of a log. "Then you dip them into this lemongrass-peanut sauce. Wow! Incredible," Besh gushes.

Some Vietnamese dishes require a bit of searching. "The one I really love, which is sometimes rare, is *bánh xèo*," says local historian Rien Fertel. *Bánh xèo*, also known as a Vietnamese crepe, is prepared by pouring rice batter with turmeric onto a hot, well-oiled skillet. The cook then tosses slivers of pork loin or pork belly, shrimp, onion, and bean sprouts onto the sizzling cake. Once the crepe is cooked, it is folded in half like an omelet. The finished dish is served with a side of lettuce, herbs, and a sweet-and-sour dipping sauce.

*Bánh xèo*, which is sold by street vendors throughout Vietnam, means "sound crepe." This delicacy received its moniker because of the popping sound the batter makes when it is poured over the piping-hot skillet. Fertel recalls the day he decided to try this dish at Magasin.

"I asked the Vietnamese waitress for a *bánh xèo*." Fertel says that she flinched with surprise. The waitress noted that most people are not familiar with the dish. "That's a dish that appeals to a lot of tastes," he adds.

Bánh xèo, *or a Vietnamese crepe, from Magasin* (Photograph by Lenny Delbert, Sr.)

Bún *(top), summer rolls (bottom left), and* phở bo *(bottom right), from Doson's Noodle House* (Photograph by Lenny Delbert, Sr.)

*Eat Well serves a vermicelli bowl with pork (bún thit    ), topped with aromatic herbs.* (Photograph by Lenny Delbert, Sr.)

For lovers of pasta, Chef Minh Bui of Café Minh recommends *bún*, the rice vermicelli. These thin, translucent noodles contain either rice or rice flour and water. The various types include *bún roi* (stirred), *bún la* (vermicelli paper), and *bún dem tram* (shredded vermicelli).

"Vermicelli is very soft and easy to eat," says Bui. He especially loves its versatility. "There are several different ways to use the *bún*," says Bui. "Grill some meat and serve it over the *bún*. Or you can put it in duck soup or chicken soup."

When it comes to trying something new, the guys from Blackened

Out Media offer a delicious recommendation. "There is this dish called *bo kho*, which is a beef stew on steroids," says writer and blogger Peter Thriffiley. A satisfying bowl of *bo kho* contains tender, slow-cooked beef, chunks of carrot, lemongrass, ginger, various spices such as cloves, and basil—topped with a touch of zesty lime juice, fresh basil, and pickled onions. Some cooks include crushed or chopped tomatoes.

"It's perfect for those cold, wintery evenings that we get twice a year in New Orleans," Thriffiley jokes. "Then you get the *bánh mì* loaves, break them apart, and dip them in there. It's just unbelievably delicious."

Rene Louapre IV likes trying new dishes but notes that some

*A hearty bowl of* bo kho (Photograph by Lenny Delbert, Sr.)

*The number nine from Nine Roses* (Photograph by Lenny Delbert)

persistence may be required. He cites an experience at Nine Roses in Gretna as an example. "I wanted the number nine," he says. This seldom-ordered dish contains slim cuts of rare beef, marinated in lemon juice and served over thinly sliced lemon and onion.

"The waitresses were reluctant to allow me to try it, because they had the belief that I'd want the *bánh mì* or *bún*," says Louapre. In the end, he enjoyed the number nine, without regrets. "It's sort of a negotiation between them and you. There's a leap of faith in pointing at something and saying: 'That's something I would like.'"

# Chapter 4

# Phở

*Phở* is essentially a type of soup, containing meat such as chicken, *phở ga*, or beef, *phở bo*. But varieties abound. A standard bowl includes long, flat rice noodles, swimming in an aromatic broth, topped with herbs and possibly hoisin and/or sriracha sauce.

*Phở*, which is heralded as the national dish of Vietnam, has

Phở bo, *or rice-noodle soup with beef, from Le Viet Café* (Photograph by Lenny Delbert, Sr.)

*A bowl of* phở *contains long, flat rice noodles, called* bánh phở. (Photograph by Lenny Delbert, Sr.)

developed a cult following here in New Orleans. Even picky eaters who are wary of exotic cuisines will try it. It is indeed a good starter dish for newcomers.

"My favorite dish, and probably the most common as well, is a great *phở*," says Chef Brian Landry. "When you find one with a great broth, and then add the bean sprouts and jalapeño, it just can't be beat."

Chef Emeril Lagasse also enjoys the popular Vietnamese dish. "I'm definitely a *phở ga* guy," he says. "I get it every time I eat Vietnamese food, which is pretty often."

Karl Takacs, Sr., the co-owner of Pho Tau Bay restaurant, recalls eating *phở* for the first time. It was the early 1970s. He was an American soldier in Vietnam, dating a young Vietnamese lady who is now his wife—Tuyett.

"Right off the bat, I loved the soup. I fell in love with it," says Takacs. "I actually made a hog of myself. I have a reputation in my father-in-law's restaurant in Saigon. I had seven bowls . . . at one time . . . one after the other . . . seven bowls." Tuyett nods her head as affirmation.

*When it comes to Vietnamese cuisine, Pho Tau Bay has been a longtime favorite of locals.* (Photograph by Lenny Delbert, Sr.)

*Karl Takacs, Sr., of Pho Tau Bay kids around with a customer.* (Photograph by Lenny Delbert, Sr.)

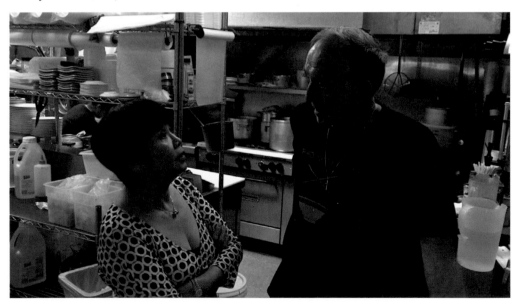

*Karl Takacs, Sr., and his wife, Tuyett* (Photograph by Lenny Delbert, Sr.)

*Karl Takacs, Jr.* (Photograph by Lenny Delbert, Sr.)

The basis of a great bowl of *phở* is the broth. While the texture of the noodles and meat, along with the freshness of the herbs, are important, the quality of the stock remains paramount. After one small spoonful, diners can determine whether or not they will have a satisfying mealtime experience.

"The heart and soul of the soup is the master stock that each chef prides himself in making," says Ian McNulty.

Because each cook employs a unique strategy to create the broth, no bowl of *phở* is the same. But there are several standard methods involved. For *phở bo,* for example, cooks usually boil a large pot of water and add beef bones, rich with marrow; chunks of beef; yellow onions; cloves; ginger; star anise; and fish sauce, among other ingredients. The ginger, along with the onions, should be toasted over an open flame before being tossed into the pot. Some cooks choose to add the chunks of beef after the broth is created.

"You have to be very patient," explains Takacs. "You start off with bone. And then you add half of your ingredients. Then you add the meat. Wait two and a half to three hours for the meat to be done. Take the meat out and add the rest of the ingredients. Take out the bones. Strain it so that the broth becomes nice and clear. And you're done."

The amount of cooking time is crucial to the finished product. Some

*Karl Takacs, Sr., prepares a batch of* phở *at Pho Tau Bay.* (Photograph by Lenny Delbert, Sr.)

chefs claim that simmering the broth for six hours is sufficient, while others aim for up to eight hours. The reason: the marrow in the bones must slowly dissolve into the water. But the result of this lengthy process is worth the wait.

The seasoned broth is poured over a heap of moist rice noodles. Diners then personalize the dish with a variety of toppings. Popular garnishes include fresh lime, mung-bean sprouts, cilantro, jalapeño, yellow onion, and Thai basil. A new dimension of flavor is provided by the addition of hoisin and/or hot sriracha sauce. Each topping serves a special purpose, such as introducing a contrast in texture or a burst of seasoning. Finding the perfect balance requires experimentation.

The origins of *phở* remain a topic of debate. But French colonization in the Far East is considered a prime influence on Vietnam's current cuisine. In fact, *phở* contains strong parallels to the French *pot au feu*, or "pot on the fire," in both taste and sound.

"The story that goes around is that this is a cross-cultural dish that the French helped found in Vietnam, during their colonial period there," says McNulty. "*Phở bo* is a beef noodle soup, similar to the *pot au feu* back in France. The *phở* is simply an adaptation, with Vietnamese tropical ingredients."

The French beef stew, which is often reserved for family feasts, contains beef, bone marrow, and chunks of carrots, turnips, celery, and onions. Cloves, salt, and pepper add spice. "In France, it's this dish that you put everything into—this big soup pot that Mama Madeleine puts her beef bones into, along with her carrots, or whatever else she has in the kitchen," explains McNulty. "And that becomes the *pot au feu*."

Other experts claim that Cantonese immigrants from the southern region of China created a type of rice-noodle soup, which evolved into the Vietnamese *phở*. Also, the soup supposedly originated in Hanoi, at the turn of the twentieth century, before spreading to other areas of the country.

"The dish is not that old," says Rien Fertel. "It's maybe less than one hundred years old. We have the soup, stock, and a bit of the beef-consumption culture from France. And then we have the noodle culture, which was well established in Vietnam before the twentieth century, from China." Fertel summarizes the theories with one concise, fitting statement. "Vietnamese cuisine, like New Orleans food—or Creole food, as we think of it—includes dishes that combine multiple cultures, multiple hands in the pot."

Although *phở* evolved from dishes already established by other cultures, it is an ideal representative of Vietnamese cuisine. It is enjoyed throughout the country, at all hours of the day—including breakfast. This Vietnamese mealtime tradition is gaining traction in

*Rien Fertel, food historian from Louisiana* (Photograph by Lenny Delbert, Sr.)

New Orleans. "*Phở* for breakfast was a new one on me," says McNulty. "I had always gone to these Vietnamese restaurants for lunch, or an early dinner, but I noticed that some of these places were open as early as seven o'clock in the morning."

McNulty jokes, "This wasn't just for them to do inventory. In Vietnam, they don't have breakfast foods like we do, such as cereal or eggs. It's not traditional. They have *phở*. And, as it turns out, it's a great way to start the day. It's very refreshing and rejuvenating. It fills you up, but it is not too heavy." McNulty has even established an annual birthday tradition of eating *phở* for breakfast, before embarking on work and celebrations.

*Phở* is an especially wise breakfast choice after a night of revelry. The aromatic broth aids in hydration. The spices allow weary diners to release toxins, through sweat. Also, this hearty meal has the same comforting effect as eating chicken noodle soup when sick.

"Vietnamese food is incredible for a hangover," says Rene Louapre. "You may crave a greasy hamburger. But *phở* is lighter. It's got more flavors and spices. It cleanses your palate. If you drink or overdrink, I recommend Vietnamese food in place of your standard hamburger."

Beginners: before you dive in, beware. Eating *phở* can be a bit tricky and messy. Maneuvering chopsticks, and pulling long noodles from broth, requires practice. First, lean closely to the bowl to minimize splashing. Grip a pair of chopsticks in one hand and a shallow spoon in the other. Gently bite the vermicelli noodles in half, and scoop the simmering broth with the spoon.

"I learned years ago with rubber bands and paper in between the chopsticks," says Andrew Gomila of Geaux Plates. "I always try to remember wearing a black shirt so that I don't get splatter on the front of me when I go eat."

Some diners save the broth for last and sip straight from the bowl. Discreetly glance around at others and mimic their approach. But it is nearly impossible to be the epitome of "grace" while slurping *phở*, so don't sweat it. Enjoy!

### PRONUNCIATION

**Blackened Out Media:**

*Rene Louapre:* I think it's "fuh." The French people say, "fuh," so I'm going to say, "fuh." But I wish I could say, "foe," because it's easier.

*Peter Thriffiley:* You sound a lot less pretentious saying, "foe."

*Louapre:* But someone will turn their nose up and say, "Y'all don't know what the hell you're talking about, because it's 'fuuuh.'"

*Vietnamese-cuisine enthusiasts Peter Thriffiley (left) and Rene Louapre* (Photograph by Lenny Delbert, Sr.)

*Randy Fertel, president of the Ruth U. Fertel Foundation, who has lectured extensively on the Vietnam War:* There's a hint of vulgarity in saying, "fuh." It sounds like you're going to say something else!

Chapter 5

# Bánh Mì

The words *bánh mì* actually refer to the type of baguette bread—
made of rice flour and wheat flour—used for this Vietnamese
sandwich. The *bánh mì* sandwich, bursting with an assortment of
flavors, is believed to be another influence of the French. The colonists
brought their baking and charcuterie traditions to Vietnam and used
the exotic produce available, rather than the standard greens that they

*An airy baguette, made with rice flour, is the basis of a* bánh mì *sandwich.*
(Photograph by Lenny Delbert, Sr.)

used back home. They began assembling a sandwich that evolved into what we now know as the *bánh mì*.

The French-Vietnamese fusion begins with airy baguette bread, coated in Vietnamese mayonnaise and either pork pâté or liver pâté. The creamy mayonnaise typically contains egg yolks, an acid, salt, and oil. It is slowly blended to perfection. The baguette cradles various cuts of meat—from charbroiled pork, or pork belly, to grilled or roasted chicken.

The finished product contains fresh sprigs of cilantro, cucumber, pickled daikon and carrot, and sliced chili peppers. The breakfast version of *bánh mì* often includes an oozing fried egg.

*Rice-flour baguettes cradle charcuterie and pickled vegetables.* (Photograph by Lenny Delbert, Sr.)

"*Bánh mì* is another example of one of those French-colonial cross-cultural things, because it's a French-bread sandwich made in a Vietnamese style, with lighter bread," says Ian McNulty. "You look inside the *bánh mì* and you have your pâté and you have the Vietnamese version of French charcuterie. On a good *bánh mì*, you open it up, and you've got three or four types of pork going on there. That seems to come straight from the French charcuterie tradition. On top of that, you have these fresh tropical vegetables that give it crunch, along with that fire from the hot peppers."

*Writer Ian McNulty has an affinity for Vietnamese cuisine.* (Photograph by Lenny Delbert, Sr.)

Though the *bánh mì* sandwich is a staple in Vietnam, it is just beginning to build a fan base across the United States. In New Orleans, it is often referred to as a Vietnamese po' boy. But even here, *bánh mì* sandwiches are prepared on light rice-flour baguettes, rather than the "French" bread used for New Orleans' renowned po' boys. But the crisp *bánh mì* baguettes create a similar effect.

"When you are talking about the baguette bread that's used for *bánh mì*, the only comparison I've seen is New Orleans po'-boy bread," says Poppy Tooker. "You don't find that delicate crumb, that light airy, weightless sort of bread, anyplace but Vietnam and New Orleans."

"Now, the traditional po'-boy maker in a New Orleans po'-boy joint would say, 'Where's the fried shrimp? Where's the gravy? Where's the debris? Where are the pickles? Where's the chopped lettuce?'" jokes McNulty. "This is a just a good way to market the *bánh mì* sandwich to new audiences."

Since eating a *bánh mì* sandwich does not require assembling a meal or fumbling with chopsticks, it is an easy way to venture into Vietnamese cuisine. And it is inexpensive yet satisfying. Newcomers usually become fans of *bánh mì* after one bite.

"I love *bánh mì*," says Chef John Besh. "On any given week, I'll stop off at Dong Phuong and pick up thirty or so and bring them to the cooks here in town. That's the way to get on the good side of your chefs," he says with a smile. "Just give them food."

Though *bánh mì* can be found at a number of Vietnamese restaurants throughout the city, many diners favor Dong Phuong Oriental Bakery and Restaurant, situated in a Vietnamese enclave in New Orleans East. Dong Phuong, which literally means "Restaurant in the East," opened in 1981.

When owners De and Huong Tran emigrated to the United States in 1980, they settled in the "Versailles" section of eastern New Orleans. De worked at a local grocery store while studying engineering, and Huong baked the pastries that she had created in her father's bakery

*Rice-flour baguettes from Dong Phuong* (Photograph by Lenny Delbert, Sr.)

back in Vietnam. Today, Dong Phuong is a bustling restaurant and bakery.

In the back of the fragrant bakery, which is crammed with colorful treats, stands a petit lady behind a deli counter that is brimming with exotic dressings and cuts of meat. She assembles sandwiches with speed and dexterity for hungry customers. The variety of *bánh mì* sandwiches sold at Dong Phuong include Vietnamese ham (*patê chả lua*), Vietnamese grilled pork (*thịt nướng xả*), barbecue chicken (*ga quay*), and vegetarian (*chay*), among others.

One Saturday morning, when Randy Fertel visited the weekly farmers' market on Alcee Fortier in New Orleans East, he stopped by Dong Phuong for a breakfast *bánh mì*. "I was standing next to my car at dawn, eating my *bánh mì*," he says. "This big Mercedes drives up. The window rolls down and this booming German voice says, 'Where is the market?' So, I pointed towards Dong Phuong. And, with my mouth full, shouted, 'And don't miss the po' boys! They're delicious!'"

The *bánh mì* has become so popular in New Orleans that non-Vietnamese restaurants serve a version of the sandwich. It is even found at a favorite local food truck—Geaux Plates. "The bayou *bánh mì* is by far our bestseller," says Andrew Gomila of Geaux Plates. "For

*A* bánh mì *is prepared in the deli section of Dong Phuong.* (Photograph by Lenny Delbert, Sr.)

our *bánh mì*, we use seven-inch baguettes from Dong Phuong Bakery in New Orleans East. We put homemade boudin sausage on the bottom. Then we add lemongrass grilled chicken, along with traditional dressings."

Though a *bánh mì* typically contains either pork pâté or liver pâté, Gomila decided to use boudin, which gives it local flavor. He notes that his unique twist on the *bánh mì* quickly became a hit. "I have a good friend who is Vietnamese," says Gomila. "She came to the food truck one of the first nights when we were open. I was worried about her reaction, but she gave me a 'thumbs up.'"

When Geaux Plates participated in the Streetfare Derby, they served the bayou *bánh mì*. It was a crowd favorite. One fest-goer took a moment to offer his opinion on this innovative sandwich. "It's spicy," he noted. "And it's got some nice flavors that just bounce around your mouth."

Geaux Plates also offers a vegetarian *bánh mì*. This sandwich still includes the traditional dressings, such as garlic-chili aioli, cucumber, cilantro, pickled chilies, and pickled carrots. But in place of meat, the *bánh mì* contains grilled eggplant, portabello mushrooms, and zucchini.

Chef Paul Artigues of Green Goddess restaurant notes that his pork belly *bánh mì* is one of the most popular items on the menu. He slathers a Dong Phuong roll with *foie gras* butter and adds cucumbers, shredded carrots, pickled turnips, sliced jalapeños, arugula, and basil.

"Then we top it off with our pork belly and shrimp, which we cook in the pork-belly juice, with Thai chili-pepper sauce. We add both crunchy and fresh green onions," he says, as he claps his hands together. "And that's about it!"

And over at Grand Isle Restaurant, Chef Mark Falgoust prepares a sandwich that is similar to the *bánh mì*—the shrimp Caminada po' boy. This indulgent Vietnamese-inspired dish took first place at the 2008 Po-Boy Festival. It contains Gulf shrimp cooked in a spicy cilantro-chili butter and covered in a slaw of Napa cabbage and carrot. Falgoust tops the shrimp and slaw with herbs, such as cilantro, parsley, and basil.

"It's not your average fried-shrimp po' boy," says Falgoust. "But everybody that gets it loves it. It's a homerun."

# Chapter 6

# Pork

Pork—often found in *bánh mì*, prepared in a variety of ways—is a primary ingredient in Vietnamese cuisine. Team March of the Pigs became a crowd favorite with their Viet Dog at the 2012 Hogs for the Cause event. Hogs for the Cause, a premier funding source for pediatric brain-cancer outreach services in the United States, sponsors

*Pork is a star in Vietnamese cuisine.* (Photograph by Rien Fertel)

a pork cook-off. At this challenging, but fun, competition, creative dishes abound.

The Viet Dog features a beloved American classic, the hot dog, with a Vietnamese twist. The sausage is made by marinating pork shoulder in a Vietnamese marinade overnight. It is then ground, cased, and grilled to order. The sausage is placed on a steamed Dong Phuong bun—shaped as a hot-dog bun, of course—and topped with slices of cucumber, jalapeño, and pickled carrots; cilantro; and a curry-mustard sauce. The co-captains of Team March of the Pigs, Andrew Shuford and Frank Palmisano, took a break from the competition to talk about the Viet Dog.

*Team March of the Pigs is a crowd favorite at Hogs.* (Photograph by Lenny Delbert, Sr.)

*The Viet Dog* (Photograph by Andrew Shuford)

After a few semesters in college, Andrew Shuford realized that he wanted to work with food and enrolled in Delgado Community College's culinary program. He graduated the month before Hurricane Katrina hit. Frank Palmisano began working in New Orleans kitchens as a way to help pay for college tuition. Since then, he has been a perpetual student of everything food and cooking.

After experiencing success at Hogs for the Cause, Shuford and Palmisano created Hoof & Cleaver, a catering company that offers whole roasted pigs. They also participate in a monthly restaurant popup at the Rusty Nail bar in the trendy Warehouse District of New Orleans. The menu is contains bar-friendly foods, including the Viet Dog.

**Suzanne Pfefferle (SP):** What is your connection to Vietnamese cuisine?

**Andrew Shuford (AS):** I was working at a restaurant in Old Metairie and my chef bought lunch, from Pho Tau Bay. I still remember I had a *báhn mì pâté thit*—fell in love before I finished the sandwich. It was the perfect blend of fatty pâté, salty ham, fresh veggies, and the spike of the jalapeño. If I had to choose a final meal, the *báhn mì pâté thit* from Pho Tau Bay would be on my wish list.

**Frank Palmisano (FP):** I developed a fondness for Vietnamese cuisine from an early age. Growing up in New Orleans, my weekends were usually spent fishing near Chef Pass in New Orleans East. Dong Phuong was a "must stop" on every fishing trip. Whether it was stuffed steam buns, croissants, or *bánh mì*, it was always delicious. As a kid, it added a dimension of foreign culinary adventure to our fishing.

**SP:** What is unique about the cuisine?

**AS:** Like a good bit of Asian cuisine, there isn't an emphasis on dairy or extremely fatty flavor, which makes it a great change of pace from a lot of traditional New Orleans or continental American cuisine. Vietnamese cuisine is still able to pack in a tremendous amount of flavor and depth, without relying on very heavy ingredients.

**FP:** The three things that stand out to me are: the abundant use of fresh vegetables, fish sauce, and its French-colonial influence. Vietnam's variety in terrain has allowed the Vietnamese to have access to a large array of tropical fruits as well as highland vegetables. Their geography also provided them with an abundant source of fresh and saltwater fish. This overabundance, of course, eventually led to a predominant culinary use of a fermented fish sauce in many of their dishes. Fish sauce gives dishes a unique flavor that's almost indescribable and is a prime example of what is referred to as "umami." While more traditional Vietnamese food can certainly stand on its own, the French occupation in the 1800s brought with it some of Europe's best culinary techniques to Vietnam.

**SP:** How did you come up with the Viet Dog concept? Describe the dish in your own words.

**AS:** For Hogs for the Cause in 2012, we were a first-time competitor that really wanted to make a splash and not just be a new kid on the block. We needed something that would appeal to festival-style eating while still being really different from your normal barbecue dish. I went back and forth about our submission with Frank, who is the co-captain of our Hogs team, and we finally settled on this great *thit*

*Andrew Shuford (left) and Frank Palmisano (right) talk about their award-winning Viet Dog.* (Photograph by Lenny Delbert, Sr.)

*nuong* [barbecue pork] recipe we got from a Vietnamese friend. The recipe was his grandmother's and we tweaked it a little bit to accent some flavor we thought should stand out.

**FP:** We wanted a festival food that was something everyone has had both a thousand times and never before. We also wanted the dish to be something other culinary professionals would recognize as a well-thought-out and executed concept.

**SP:** What was the response at Hogs for the Cause?

**AS:** Great! "Hogs" is my favorite festival in New Orleans because the organizers [Becker Hall and Rene Louapre IV] really want the teams involved to showcase the interesting side of pork, not just barbecue. People come in expecting to see some interesting stuff and we definitely were the benefactors of that expectation in 2012. People loved the concept of a traditional American street food with all the flavor of Vietnamese classics. We sold over 250 at Hogs in 2012.

**FP:** Everyone really loved it! It was something that was familiar enough for people to try and have fun with. The green steamed bun was a real crowd pleaser with the festival-goers. It won second place in the creative foods category amongst fifty other competitors.

**SP:** How have fans of the Hoof & Cleaver whole-hog catering company (which is also a restaurant popup) reacted?

**AS:** Very well. The great thing about popups is that they allow you to have direct contact with your customers and get very direct feedback. People are still intrigued by Vietnamese food and love the crossover appeal of the dish.

**FP:** We sold out within a few hours.

**SP:** Do you see the trend continuing?

**AS:** There are so many variations and family recipes that make every dish a little different that it is impossible to try everything or grow tired of the cuisine. In addition, there is a dish for every season—spring rolls and vermicelli salads with fresh veggies during the hot months, rice platters in the fall, and there is nothing better than the delicious bowl of *bo kho* during the first cold snap of the winter.

**FP:** The trend is just getting started. As people gravitate to healthier food options, Vietnamese cuisine provides a new and exotic dining alternative with a flavorful, guilt-free experience.

# Chapter 7

# Beverages

"I think that soda *chan* is an overlooked beverage," says Peter Thriffiley. "It tastes more refreshing than Pepsi or Coca-Cola. It's delicious."

This refreshing drink consists of lime juice, soda water, and sugar.

*Soda* chan *is served at Doson's Noodle House.* (Photograph by Lenny Delbert, Sr.)

And it is easy to assemble. Simply add the ingredients to a glass of ice, and stir.

Rene Louapre opts for an icy beer. "Some things go better with cold beer. With Vietnamese food, you have all these different flavors going on," Louapre says. "The beer kind of cleanses your palate, revives you, and gets you ready for that next bite."

The beers that are most prevalent in Vietnam can be found in a number of local Vietnamese restaurants. Singha®, which is a pale lager made by the Boon Rawd Brewery in Thailand, has become an international favorite. Tiger Beer®, from Singapore, is another popular pale lager. Launched in 1932, it is served in more than sixty countries today and is consumed throughout Vietnam.

In addition to selecting a drink for meal pairings, diners can enjoy a number of sweet beverages for dessert—assuming they have room for dessert. Bubble tea, also known as *boba* tea, is a thick, sweet Vietnamese beverage that begins with a base of black or green tea and fruit. The choice of fruit flavors includes strawberry, peach, kiwi, and pineapple.

The frosty concoction also contains chewy tapioca balls. Tapioca, or *bột năng*, is essentially starch, extracted from a cassava plant. The thick tapioca balls—slurped through a wide plastic straw—serve no nutritional purpose but add texture. In place of tapioca balls, some eateries use shredded strips of jelly in such flavors as coconut and mango.

Bubble tea often, but not always, includes milk. The ingredients are either stirred and poured over ice or blended together into a smoothie-like shake.

Some dulcet drinks are a bit more exotic for Western diners. Tiffany Le of Le Viet Café serves a refreshing beverage that is indigenous to Vietnam. *Sâm bổ lượng* contains Job's-tears, dried longans, red jujubes, lotus seeds, thinly sliced seaweed, strips of ginger, ginkgo nuts, water, sugar, and crushed ice. Alternate ingredients may be used to create a similar effect. *Sâm bổ lượng,* which is also known as *che sâm bổ lượng,* loosely means "sweet soup." The name is fitting, since a spoon is required to fetch the ingredients that are floating throughout the tall glass of ice.

But one beverage in particular is experiencing a surge in popularity—*cà phê sữa đá* also known as a Vietnamese iced coffee. This jolting, caffeinated concoction is found throughout Vietnam. Now available at many local restaurants and coffee shops, the drink is establishing a strong presence in the coffee-loving culture of New Orleans.

"Basically if you look at the words *cà phê,* it's coffee," says Ian McNulty.

Sâm bổ lượng *(back center) from Le Viet Café* (Photograph by Lenny Delbert, Sr.)

*Hot water is poured over coffee grinds to create a* cà phê sữa đá. (Photograph by Lenny Delbert, Sr.)

*Slow-dripped coffee is the basis of a* cà phê sữa đá. (Photograph by Lenny Delbert, Sr.)

*A* cà phê sữa đá *from Antoine's Annex* (Photograph by Lenny Delbert, Sr.)

"In addition to having a great baking culture in Vietnam, they have a coffee culture as well."

*Cà phê sữa đá* contains strong coffee slowly dripped over a glass of ice. Sometimes a generous portion of condensed milk sits at the bottom of the glass. The hot coffee melts some of the ice and mingles with the milk, resulting in a sweet, invigorating coffee drink.

"Ironically, here in New Orleans, a lot of Vietnamese restaurants that make *cà phê sữa đá* use a very familiar local brand—Café du Monde—which is the old French Market coffee brand," adds McNulty. "The Vietnamese that I've spoken with say it's the closest they can find to what they would traditionally use back home."

Though *cà phê sữa đá* is commonly found at Vietnamese restaurants in the New Orleans area, coffee shops such as Antoine's Annex in the French Quarter also serve the drink. With its burgeoning popularity, Vietnamese iced coffee will surely become a staple in the New Orleans coffee scene.

# Chapter 8

# Vietnamese Baking Traditions

Just as non-Vietnamese chefs in New Orleans have developed an affinity for Vietnamese dishes and incorporate the cuisine into their menus, the local Vietnamese have mastered the art of baking. Establishments such as Café du Monde bustle with Vietnamese cooks. Young Vietnamese waiters and waitresses waltz through the crowded seating area, carrying heavy trays laden with hot beignets. And Vietnamese-owned bakeries—from Dong Phuong and Chez Pierre to Hi-Do and O'Delice—have become local favorites.

Hi-Do Bakery on Terry Parkway on the West Bank is renowned for its old-style Mardi Gras king cakes, a recognizable icon of New Orleans. The demand for these dulcet cakes continues to grow. "I think that is the best bakery in the city," says Mark Falgoust of Grand Isle Restaurant. "It's a small, family-oriented bakery that pays attention to detail. They take pride in their work and it shows." Falgoust recommends that first-time visitors try the bear claws.

But Hi-Do is best known for their cinnamon-flavored king cakes. These light, and not overly sweet, cakes come covered in purple, green, and gold sprinkles—sans the oozing white icing. They can be ordered in shapes symbolic of New Orleans, such as a fleur de lis or crawfish.

Another Vietnamese-owned eatery is O'Delice French Bakery and Pastries on Magazine Street in Uptown. Established in 2004, the small

*Young Vietnamese waiters and waitresses serve beignets at Café du Monde.*
(Photograph by Lenny Delbert, Sr.)

*Hi-Do Bakery offers traditional king cakes and an assortment of dulcet delights.*
(Photograph by Lenny Delbert, Sr.)

*King cakes are baked at Hi-Do Bakery.* (Photograph by Lenny Delbert, Sr.)

bakery serves sweet delicacies, made from scratch. "O'Delice has, by far, been one of my favorite destinations for king cake," says Rien Fertel. "It's the best. I go through about a dozen during Carnival season."

Besides king cakes, the bakery creates an assortment of cookies, such as M&M and macadamia nut. And the variety of cakes ranges from praline cheesecake and German chocolate to carrot and coconut cream. For a snack, select a fresh-fruit tart or cream-filled éclair.

Despite the assortment of bakery options in New Orleans, diners continue flock to Dong Phuong Bakery. In addition to offering traditional French pastries such as croissants and macaroons, Dong

*Dong Phuong is known for its light baguette bread, among other baked goods.* (Photograph by Lenny Delbert, Sr.)

*Sweet treats from Dong Phuong* (Photograph by Lenny Delbert, Sr.)

Phuong carries Vietnamese desserts. For a Far East experience, try the steamed banana with sticky rice (*bánh chuoi nep*), mung-bean pies (*bánh đâu xanh nướng*), or sweet-corn dessert cup (*băp chè*) with coconut syrup. You may feel as though you've been transported to a bustling Saigon café.

# Chapter 9

# Urban Farms and Aquaponics

"Coming to America, I remember, we were in my uncle's boat, because we lived in a fishing village in Vietnam," says Tiffany Le. "We were in the middle of the water. There were soldiers on both

*Tiffany Le is the owner of Le Viet Café on St. Charles Avenue.* (Photograph by Lenny Delbert, Sr.)

sides, shooting. The next thing I remember, there's this huge American ship, picking us up. And they pick us up like a net—scooped us up." Before arriving in New Orleans, Le briefly lived in Missouri.

Fr. Vien Nguyen fled Vietnam a few months before the fall of Saigon. He arrived in Arkansas in 1977. "There was a lot of uncertainty," he says. "We didn't know where we were going. So we [his family] basically just followed the crowd." Because of his Catholicism, Nguyen moved to New Orleans—a city that is heavily populated by Catholics.

The late Archbishop Philip Hannan of New Orleans, a descendant of Irish immigrants, understood the importance of keeping the Vietnamese refugees together, rather than dispersing them throughout the city. He also knew that Catholics have a tendency to gather around their priest. So Hannan visited Vietnamese refugee camps throughout the region and invited them to come to New Orleans East. He then acquired subsidized apartments there that would accommodate large families. With their meager possessions, the refugees moved into their new neighborhood—what is now Village de l'Est—and began rebuilding their lives.

Despite the assumption that the Vietnamese chose to live in New Orleans because of the tropical climate, reminiscent of their homeland, they relocated here because of the availability of land and housing. The fact that Village de l'Est is situated near the Maxent Lagoon enabled the refugees to mimic the kind of life, in terms of agriculture, that they experienced in Vietnam.

"That's how we ended up in New Orleans East," says Nguyen. "That's how we ended up in Algiers. That's how we ended up in Harvey. We chose that place because there's an availability of apartments where a lot of people could gather and felt at home."

Chef Minh Bui notes that he, along with other refugees, clicked into survival mode. "We didn't have much in our hands to work with," he says. "The people in our Catholic community would tell each other,

*Archbishop Hannan helped find housing for Vietnamese War refugees.* (Photograph courtesy of the *Clarion Herald*)

'We have to work with what God gives to us.' We did it. Take what you have and work with it."

The New Orleans East Vietnamese community established grocery stores, restaurants, and a church—Mary Queen of Vietnam—where Nguyen served as priest. Soon, Village de l'Est was thriving. In that area as well as the West Bank, where there was unused land, the Vietnamese began growing vegetable and fruit gardens.

"We are very much an agricultural people," says Nguyen. "So as we arrived, we looked around for seeds for the plants, vegetables,

*The backyard edible gardens in Village de l'Est are abundant with leafy greens.* (Photograph by Lenny Delbert, Sr.)

*Vibrant-hued dragon fruit from Hong Kong Market on the West Bank* (Photograph by Lenny Delbert, Sr.)

the fruits that we grew in Vietnam. And we grew them around our houses."

Following Hurricane Katrina, the urban gardens expanded out of necessity. The Vietnamese had returned to their homes immediately after the storm, but the places that provided food resources—such as the local supermarket—were still out of commission. The community realized that, if another disaster occurred, they must be able to supply their own food.

*Fr. Vien Nguyen, the former priest of Mary Queen of Vietnam, was instrumental in increasing the use of urban gardens and initiating a business partnership with John Besh.* (Photograph by Lenny Delbert, Sr.)

Many of the Vietnamese who lost their jobs and homes were unable to receive assistance from relief programs because they did not speak English. The Mary Queen of Vietnam Community Development Corporation, Inc. (MQVNCDC) was established in 2006 to help these families. "When you rely on someone else, you are at that person's mercy. So we no longer want to rely completely on others," says Nguyen.

Nguyen and others from the community joined forces with Chef John Besh, in an effort to amplify the use of urban gardens and generate a financial reward for community, which would ultimately boost the local economy. "What we wanted to do is this: every dollar

*Lemongrass grows in an urban garden.* (Photograph by Lenny Delbert, Sr.)

that we spend, let's try to spend it locally," says Besh. "And so if we can spend it with the community in New Orleans East, then we are not only helping them, but we are helping the city grow. We're helping the economy recover from Katrina."

Besh continues, "If I could expose the Vietnamese farmers to the type of produce that we use the most of [in his restaurants], then we could buy the seeds. They could plant them and tend to them. We would buy the crops back." Besh notes that the partnership has been a fruitful one—for both groups.

But rather than using one large plot of land for a farm, which may eventually happen, individual households create edible gardens in

*A Vietnamese couple tends to their edible garden.* (Photograph by Lenny Delbert, Sr.)

their own backyards. In a typical tract, neat rows of bright cabbage flutter in the breeze and beets sprout from the ground, along with bundles of lemongrass and fragrant cilantro. Farmers snip small berries from a branch, scrape dirt from sweet potatoes plucked from the earth, and delicately drop plump tomatoes into a bin. Some backyards even boast aloe plants.

"It was so mesmerizing to see not only the fruit and vegetables grown in these backyards but the economy of use of space," says Poppy Tooker. "I don't think that the Vietnamese people see any use in a lawn. They are so far ahead of us in this new trend towards urban agriculture, where it is much smarter to grow something edible instead of St. Augustine grass. Every square inch was occupied with something growing something delicious, exotic herb varieties," she adds. "Breadfruit. That was my big takeaway. That's like right out of Rodgers and Hammerstein's *South Pacific!*"

With the help of the MQVNCDC, residents of Village de l'Est have also developed an aquaponics system. This sustainable food-production system combines traditional aquaculture—raising aquatic animals, such as koi fish—with hydroponics. Hydroponics allows the cultivation of plants in water, in a symbiotic environment.

Many of the refugees who moved to New Orleans during the fall of Saigon were from fishing families. They settled along the Gulf Coast, particularly in Plaquemines Parish, purchased boats, and searched for business opportunities. The Vietnamese became successful in earning an income at sea, as they did back home.

Today, of the 40,000 Vietnamese in the Gulf Coast region, one out of three works in the seafood industry. Shrimp boats, which are shared by family members, are passed down from one generation to the next. "The Vietnamese influence on the shrimping industry is a vital one," says Chef Brian Landry. "Shrimping is the single most important fishing industry in Louisiana. Traditionally, it's been a generational call to arms for families. But as some of those family-run shrimping

*Daniel Nguyen, of the MQVNCDC, explains the aquaponics process.* (Photograph by Lenny Delbert, Sr.)

*This view of a coast in Vietnam affirms that fishing is a way of life for many Vietnamese.* (Photograph by Rien Fertel)

*In the coastal cities of Vietnam, varieties of fresh fish are abundant.* (Photograph by Neil Alexander)

businesses have disappeared, the Vietnamese people have stepped in to help keep that industry going."

From the Vietnamese who fish for oysters, shrimp, and crabs to those who package seafood, many found themselves without a source of income after the BP oil spill in 2010. "At the time of the BP oil spill, I believe 44 percent of the fishing vessels in the Gulf Coast were owned by Vietnamese Americans," says Nguyen. "So imagine the repercussions on those who make their living at sea or way back at the wharf. Imagine the rippling effect. Everything came to a screeching halt."

So they scrambled to find a solution to this dire situation. The aquaponics system employed by the MQVNCDC acted as an

*The Vietnamese play a significant role in the Gulf Coast shrimping industry.* (Photograph by Lenny Delbert, Sr.)

agricultural and aquacultural alternative, allowing the community to create a safe, environmentally and economically sustainable seafood-production system.

"When it's something like an oil spill, we can't control it," says Nguyen. "But if we were to grow our crops, through the aquaponics system, we would alleviate the burden of relying on the sea. At the same time, we would have more control over the food that we consume and sell."

Rather than purchasing such items as dried shrimp and fish sauce from places such as Thailand and China, Nguyen and members of the MQVNCDC aim to utilize local resources. "The people from my community have the skills to create these items," he says. "If we were to do it here, it would help in terms of job creation. We can also control the quality of the food."

In addition to the aquaponics system and training center at the MQVNCDC headquarters on Alcee Fortier Boulevard, aquaponics systems have been established in backyards throughout Village de l'Est. With aquaponics, the MQVNCDC grows basil mint, kale, spinach, tomatoes, cucumbers, lettuce, cilantro, basil, and strawberries, among other produce.

MQVNCDC is in the process of developing a Growers Cooperative to sell locally produced vegetables to metropolitan markets, such as the Hollygrove Market, along with numerous restaurants throughout the Greater New Orleans area, which would lead to an increase in commercial sales.

# Chapter 10

# Asian Markets

*Outdoor markets in Vietnam are brimming with fresh produce.* (Photograph by Rien Fertel)

Members of the Village de l'Est community have not strayed far from the shopping habits that they practiced back in their homeland. Crops grown in the backyard gardens are sold at a weekly farmers' market located in an empty parking lot alongside Alcee Fortier Boulevard, in New Orleans East. "We call it the squatting market, meaning that our people—the sellers—just squat on the ground," says Fr. Vien Nguyen. "And then the buyers come and evaluate the products and bargain. So it's very much like Vietnam."

Vietnamese women wearing conical harvesting hats roll out blankets and cover them with bundles of produce—from cabbage to carrots to cucumbers—for display. Large ice chests cradle fresh seafood, caught during the early-morning hours. Ducks and chickens scramble around in closed-off areas. Exotic items, such as dragon fruit, can be purchased,

*The steps for purchasing products at the Alcee Fortier farmers' market are similar to the process in Vietnam.* (Photograph by Neil Alexander)

but they disappear quickly. The sellers negotiate with customers—in fast Vietnamese, of course. Once the price is agreed, cash is exchanged between the two parties.

"The Saturday farmers' market out in Village de l'Est is just magical," says Ian McNulty. "You have to go very early. If you get there at 8:00 A.M., it is slim pickings. So, to make this trek, you get up fishing-trip early—the crack of dawn. When you get there, it looks like you are right smack dab in the Far East."

"The Saturday market in New Orleans East is probably the one I

*In addition to fresh produce, livestock can be purchased at the Saturday farmers' market.* (Photograph by Lenny Delbert, Sr.)

visit most," says Chef John Besh. He arrives around five o'clock in the morning and scoops up an assortment of vegetables and herbs. Afterwards, he heads to Dong Phuong for breakfast and buys cream-filled pastries "to go" for his family.

"You wouldn't expect to see this in New Orleans," says Besh. "It's reminiscent of one of the great markets in Chinatown anywhere else in the country, whether it be New York or San Francisco. I can get a huge bunch of cilantro or lemongrass, for a buck or two, along with incredible chicken eggs. Duck eggs are a hot commodity."

Markets are also gathering points for members of the close-knit

Vietnamese community. Nguyen notes that, after Katrina, residents frequently inquired about the status of the market. The market was urgently needed not only for its locally grown produce but because it was a venue for community members to meet and discuss the events of the previous week.

"We don't really have public space for them to gather," says Nguyen. "We have the church. But people go there for worship. We have buildings. But that's for meetings. But just to hang loose, that [the market] is the only place, really."

"The very best markets are not just about acquiring ingredients,"

*A woman sells her homegrown produce at the Saturday-morning farmers' market on Alcee Fortier Boulevard.* (Photograph by Lenny Delbert, Sr.)

says Poppy Tooker. "They are about creating a community. That's exactly what's going on at those Vietnamese farmers' markets."

But not everyone attends the weekly market. "They open awfully early—five in the morning," says Tiffany Le. "That's when the dreaming is good!"

Those who prefer to shop at a more convenient hour can visit the massive Hong Kong Food Market, housed in an old Walmart building on the West Bank. Tooker frequents this market for both the array of Asian food items and the reasonable prices. "The first thing that catches your attention, aside from the sheer quantity of available food, is the low prices," she says.

*A variety of meat products, including pork, can be found at Hong Kong Market.* (Photograph by Lenny Delbert, Sr.)

Tooker continues, "The seafood is so fresh. And there is an old classic that you rarely see—pompano en papillote. This old French classic is an expensive dish to cook, unless you know to go buy your pompano at the Hong Kong Food Market."

"It's an incredible experience," says Rene Louapre of Blackened Out Media. He also points out that the Hong Kong Food Market is a good place to spot some of the city's best chefs. During their off hours, many of the most talented men and women of New Orleans' culinary scene frequent this market.

Louapre recommends first stopping at the *phở* restaurant situated at

*The produce section of Hong Kong Market boasts an abundance of leafy greens, such as bok choy.* (Photograph by Lenny Delbert, Sr.)

the entrance of the Hong Kong Food Market, to avoid shopping on an empty stomach. "That way, you won't buy everything on the shelves and come out with squid balls and all the other things that they sell. But it's really great exposure to the flavors and the vegetables and the herbs of Asian cooking."

When Andrew Gomila of Geaux Plates visits the Hong Kong Food Market, he usually walks out with items he has never seen before—even if the label is not in English. He enjoys experimenting with new, unknown foods. "Sometimes it's a spectacular failure," says Gomila. "Sometimes it works out great."

"I'll get a few produce items, like chilies that you cannot find at other stores," says Mark Falgoust of Grand Isle Restaurant. Rather than visiting the Hong Kong Food Market with a recipe in mind, he selects food items on a whim. "There are so many different chili options. But you have to watch out, because some are really spicy."

Chapter 11

# Family Traditions and *Tết* Festival

Because the Vietnamese community is so close-knit, with families still sitting down together for each meal, its culinary traditions have remained intact. And prior to the actual meal, family members spend time in the kitchen, sharing the preparation responsibilities. The recipes that lead to a lively feast have been passed from one generation to the next.

"These are people who sit down to eat multiple meals a day," says Poppy Tooker. "These folks are not just eating dinner together. They're having breakfast together. When you're keeping a family unit together, around a table, then the food is paramount. I think that that is why their cuisine has remained in such pure condition."

"My dad would do the blessing before we all sit down to eat lunch, dinner, or breakfast," says Tiffany Le. "After my dad does the blessing, we eat." Le explains that a traditional Vietnamese dinner often includes up to five courses, beginning with a soup and salad, followed by stir-fry, fish, and a type of meat.

Though Joseph Cao enjoys dinner with his wife and two young daughters, they often eat late, after they have completed an activity-filled day. "We have a mixture of American food as well as Vietnamese food," he says. "It's just a time for us to get together, sit, and chat and discuss the day."

Mealtime traditions are especially lively during the week of *Tết Nguyên Đán*, usually referred to as *Tết*—the Vietnamese lunar new

*Joseph Cao, former U.S. Congressman for Louisiana and owner of the Cao Law Firm.*
(Photograph by Lenny Delbert, Sr.)

year. This annual celebration begins on the first day of the first month
of the lunar calendar, which is usually late January or early February,
and ends on the third day. Customs include visiting family members,
saying prayers to deceased ancestors, cleaning the house, wearing
new clothes, and—of course—preparing festive delicacies.

"The first of the year, all of the children and grandchildren would
gather at the patriarch or the matriarch's home," explains Fr. Vien
Nguyen. And then the next day, we would go to mass, specifically
to pray for the deceased. On the third day, you bring good wishes to
your teachers or those who are at higher ranking, in terms of family

*Families in the Vietnamese community maintain strong mealtime traditions, especially during the week of* Tết. (Photograph by Lenny Delbert, Sr.)

relatives. But all of that involves food and lots of cheerful noises. It's very loud."

One treat, normally reserved for *Tết*, is *bánh chưng*. This sweet rice cake, which is shaped as a square, is sometimes filled with mung-bean paste and barbecue pork. But preparation requires patience. *Bánh chưng* takes up to five hours to create. In Nguyen's family, the preparation process became a tradition in itself.

The method begins by setting the sticky rice onto a banana leaf, covering it with a layer of mung-bean paste and pork, and wrapping it into the shape of a square. The packet is placed into boiling water.

Water must continuously be added during the cooking process, so that the *bánh chưng* does not burn.

"For us young people, that is when we would promise each other that we would stay up all night just to watch," says Nguyen. "But, of course, we would doze off after a couple of hours. But that is part of the tradition, where the family gathers not only in the dining area but also in the kitchen."

For the local Vietnamese community, the major *Tết* gathering takes place at Mary Queen of Vietnam, in New Orleans East. Vietnamese pop singers warble songs for fest-goers, children play darts and toss ping-pong balls into glass fishbowls, and colorful dragon dancers hop

*A young girl celebrates* Tết *with her family.* (Photograph by Lenny Delbert, Sr.)

*During* Tết, *fans of Vietnamese cuisine can sample an array of tasty items.* (Photograph by Lenny Delbert, Sr.)

along the stage as incandescent fireworks explode in a kaleidoscope of colors across the sky. Exotic food—to Westerners, at least—abounds. In one section of the festival grounds, a crowd congregates under a massive tent, carrying trays laden with steaming bowls of *phở*. In another area, women deftly prepare *bánh mì* and wrap *gỏi cuốn* for customers. Some adventurous eaters dine on duck eggs.

"It is this big festival where food is the real centerpiece," says John Besh. "And it's not the hog slaughtered. It's actually the goat. And you

*New Orleanians feast on* phở *at the annual* Tết *festival.* (Photograph by Lenny Delbert, Sr.)

can eat curried goat. But you also get some of the best seafood in the country—right there in New Orleans East. It was not inconceivable, because it is very similar to the culture of South Louisiana, where we are family and community oriented. We are always gathering around food."

# Chapter 12

# Younger Generations of Vietnamese Americans

The traditions of Vietnamese culture have been passed down to the younger generations of the Vietnamese American community. Although these younger generations have become intertwined with the New Orleans community and culture, they proudly embrace their heritage.

As a child, Chef John Besh worked in the kitchen with protective Vietnamese immigrants, following the fall of Saigon. Today, he collaborates in the culinary world with their children, mindful of preserving their heritage. "The first people off the boat, who are working in restaurants and on the shrimp boats, have children that have gone to college and become professionals," Besh says.

He staunchly believes that the ability of the Vietnamese to overcome major obstacles is due to their emphasis on family and faith. "I think that there's a lot that we can all learn by the way that the Vietnamese have not just lived and survived here but how they have thrived here," says Besh.

The Vietnamese youth played an integral role in reviving their community post-Katrina—whether it involved translating news reports into Vietnamese or filling out paperwork in English. "Now they are being appreciated," says Fr. Vien Nguyen. "What I find is that our youth are proud of the fact that they are Vietnamese Americans."

Joseph Cao reminds his two daughters, who were both raised in New Orleans, to embrace their Vietnamese traditions. "We try very much to keep some elements of the Vietnamese culture," he says. "We try to encourage our young people to be proud of the heritage and to be proud of who they are."

Organizations such as the Vietnamese Young Leaders Association of New Orleans allow the adolescents and young adults of the Vietnamese community to come together, collaborate, and celebrate their heritage. VAYLA, which is based in New Orleans, provides a social and educational forum for Vietnamese Americans.

Though the Vietnamese Americans maintain their family and cultural traditions, they have intermingled with mainstream society. A peek into an Uptown coffee shop, popular festival, or college campus provides proof. They represent their rich heritage, and the city of New Orleans, with aplomb.

Each year, the Loyola Asian Student Organization at Loyola University hosts a cooking competition. During this spirited event, Asian clubs from Tulane University, Xavier University, and the University of New Orleans, among other local colleges, compete in front of a panel of renowned local chefs. When Chef John Besh attended the competition, he was caught by surprise.

"I'm not eating all day, thinking I'm going to have this Vietnamese feast," he says. "And [I] go, and what do I have? I have the foods that I grew up with. I had shrimp Creole. I had red beans and rice. It was the same food, just done differently. Lemongrass showed up here; basil mint was added there. But when I think about it, the people in this competition are just as much of a New Orleanian as I am and just as much of a Louisianian as I am."

Ian McNulty believes that the burgeoning popularity of exotic fare is not merely a culinary trend. "We have a lot of homegrown talent. We have this second, third, and fourth generation of Vietnamese people that want to go out and do their own thing," he says. "And they are not necessarily going to do it the way that their grandparents did it. They are going to make it a little more hip, a little more accessible to people their age, from a broader spread of New Orleans."

*College students create Asian-inspired delights at a cooking competition hosted by Loyola University in New Orleans.* (Photograph by Lenny Delbert, Sr.)

The large Vietnamese population in New Orleans provides an ideal base for the cuisine to grow. And the younger generations of Vietnamese Americans will continue to take it to new levels, while retaining the trademarks that make it unique. As for the local Vietnamese, both young and old? Their dynamic culture—from their work ethic, emphasis on family, and eternal optimism—has been embraced, and always will be appreciated, by the city. For that, I extend to them a heartfelt *"cám ơn"* (thank you).

Chapter 13

# Recipes

*Crispy Salt and Pepper Squid, from Ba Mien* (Photograph by Ba Mien)

107

# Crispy Salt and Pepper Squid

*Ba Mien*

Vegetable oil for frying
1 cup self-rising flour
1 tbsp. garlic powder
1 tsp. ground pepper
1 lb. squid, cut into 1½-in. squares
　and scored for even cooking
1 tsp. soy sauce
2 tbsp. sweet chili sauce

1 tsp. oyster sauce
1 tbsp. butter
1 tbsp. vegetable oil
½ cup chopped green bell pepper
½ cup chopped red bell pepper
½ cup chopped onion
2 jalapeños, sliced
2 cloves garlic, sliced

Heat a pot of vegetable oil to 350 degrees.

Combine the flour, garlic powder, and pepper in a shallow bowl. Then dredge the squid in the flour, shaking off the excess. Drop the squid in the hot oil, piece by piece to avoid sticking together. Cook for about 1-2 minutes until light brown. Then remove the squid from the oil and place on paper towels to drain.

In a small bowl, mix together the soy, sweet chili, and oyster sauce. Set aside.

In a wok or large skillet, melt the butter and oil together on medium heat. Then add the bell peppers, onion, jalapeños, and garlic. Stir fry until soft, about 1-2 minutes.

Turn heat up to medium high, then add the fried squid and toss to incorporate all of the flavors. Lastly, pour the sauce all over the squid and toss to coat. Serve immediately. Serves 4.

# Sautéed Lobster Tail
*Tan Dinh*

2 whole lobsters, about 2 lb. each
2 tsp. vegetable oil
1 tsp. diced garlic
¼ cup chopped white onion
¼ cup chopped green onion
1 lime
¼ cup fish sauce

3 tsp. sugar
¼ cup butter
1 tsp. cornstarch
1 tsp. pepper
1 tsp. salt
½ can Coco Rico soda

The lobsters may be alive/fresh or can be steamed before starting the recipe. If they are steamed beforehand, be sure to reserve the lobster juice from the heads.

To make the lobster sauce, heat oil in pan. Add garlic and white onion. Sauté.

Add green onion. Sauté for 3 minutes. Squeeze lime juice over mixture and add reserved lobster juice from the heads. Simmer.

Add fish sauce, sugar, 1 tsp. butter, 1 tsp. cornstarch, 1 tsp. pepper, and 1 tsp. salt. Add Coco Rico. Let the ingredients simmer and set aside.

Sauté whole tails in remaining butter, only until butter melts and is absorbed by the meat. Add the lobster sauce. Serve with rice or as an appetizer with garlic bread.

# Vietnamese Spring Roll (Shrimp)

*Le Viet Café*

Rice paper
Bibb lettuce
Rice noodles, cooked according to
    pkg. instructions
Bean sprouts

Julienned cucumbers
Shrimp, boiled or sautéed
Basil leaves
Mint leaves
Cilantro leaves

Dip the rice paper in warm water. Rice paper is delicate and only needs a quick dip in warm water to soften. Do not "soak" the rice paper for too long because it will break down, making the rolling more difficult.

Lay slightly firm rice paper down on a board and start assembling ingredients for the filling. During the time that you assemble ingredients, the rice paper will become soft and gelatinous.

Starting at top ⅓ of rice paper, lay down lettuce first—this will prevent any sharp fillings from tearing the soft rice paper. Make sure to lay the fillings at the top ⅓ to leave plenty of surface area to roll. The more rotations of rice paper you have, the stronger it will be and less likely to puncture.

Add the remaining filling ingredients, in the order listed. Do not overstuff the roll. Start small and add more fillings that work with the size of the rice paper.

Gently pull the top edge of the rice paper away from the work surface and roll over the filling. At the same time, use your forefingers to gather and "tuck" the fillings together under the paper. "Tucking" keeps the fillings together and tight, so that the roll remains firm and straight. Continue to "roll and tuck" forward.

*Peanut Sauce*

¾ cup natural-style creamy peanut
   butter
⅓ cup water
3 tbsp. hoisin sauce
1 tbsp. sugar

2¼ tsp. garlic-chili paste
1 medium garlic clove, mashed
½ cup coconut milk
4 tbsp. chopped green onion
2 tbsp. chopped white onion

    Mix the sauce ingredients and serve in a small bowl alongside the roll.

# Grilled Pork Vermicelli

*Eat Well*

3 tbsp. soy sauce
1 tbsp. fish sauce
⅛ cup minced red onion
¼ cup minced garlic
½ cup minced lemongrass
3 tbsp. cracked black pepper

2 tbsp. sesame oil
8 tbsp. Lee Kum Kee Char Siu Sauce
2 tbsp. cooking wine
2 tbsp. honey
3 lb. pork shoulder

Mix all ingredients except pork. Pour over meat, and marinate for at least 4 hours in the refrigerator. Grill over medium heat, basting with marinade, for 10-15 minutes. Using a meat thermometer, cook until pork reaches a temperature of 185 degrees.

Remove pork. Place onto platter, and let rest for 10-20 minutes. Thinly slice.

## Vermicelli

1 pkg. rice vermicelli

Cook vermicelli in boiling water until tender. Rinse under cold water and drain before serving with the meat.

## Sauce

| | |
|---|---|
| 1 cup sugar | 3 cups water |
| 1 cup fish sauce | Juice of 3 limes |

Bring ingredients to a boil. Let cool.

Place pork on vermicelli. Drizzle with some of the sauce. Add fresh minced garlic and minced red Thai chili pepper, according to taste. Can also be served with julienned cucumber, shredded lettuce, and cilantro.

# Fr. Vien's Chicken Salad

*Brian Landry, Borgne*

*Shredded Chicken*

Two 2- to 3-lb. chickens, preferably
 kosher or free range
Kosher salt and freshly ground
 black pepper to taste
4 tbsp. turmeric
8 slices ginger, peeled and cut into
 ¼-in.-thick pieces

4 stalks lemongrass, chopped
1 bunch green onions, white and
 green parts, thinly sliced
½ cup Thai basil
4 qt. water

Season the chickens inside and out with salt, pepper, and turmeric. In a pot large enough to hold the chickens completely submerged in liquid, combine the chickens, breast sides up, with the ginger, lemongrass, green onions, basil, and water. Bring to a low simmer over medium heat.

Reduce the heat to low and simmer for 45-60 minutes. The chickens are done when the meat can be easily removed from the bones. Remove the chickens from the pot, and allow to cool enough to handle. Separate the chicken from the bones. Remove the skin from the chickens and shred the meat.

## Salad

6 cups thinly sliced cabbage
1 cup mint leaves
1 cup basil leaves
1 cup cilantro leaves
2 cups pickled carrot sticks

18 Bibb lettuce cups
12 tbsp. chopped roasted peanuts
30 slices pickled jalapeño
3 tbsp. fried garlic chips

Mix chicken, cabbage, herbs, and carrots in a mixing bowl. Divide the lettuce cups among 6 plates, and fill the cups with the chicken and cabbage mixture. Using 12 oz. of the dipping fish sauce, dress the lettuce cups with the dipping fish sauce, and garnish with peanuts, jalapeños, and garlic chips. Serves 6.

## Dipping Fish Sauce

4 cups fish sauce
2 cups water
1 cup rice wine vinegar
Juice of 6 limes

2 cups sugar
3 tbsp. minced garlic
2 bird's-eye chilis, thinly sliced

In a large mixing bowl, combine all ingredients and whisk thoroughly until sugar dissolves.

# Black and Blue Crab Fingers

*Brian Landry, Borgne*

1 tbsp. minced garlic
1 tbsp. minced ginger
1 tbsp. minced shallot
2 tsp. sesame oil
¼ cup rice wine
2 qt. crab stock
1 tbsp. soy sauce
1 tbsp. fish sauce
2 tbsp. hoisin sauce

2 tbsp. oyster sauce
1 tsp. Szechuan peppercorns
¼ cup cornstarch
1½ tbsp. cracked black pepper
2 lb. blue crab fingers
2 cups rice flour
Vegetable oil for frying
6 cups steamed white rice

Sweat the garlic, ginger, and shallot in sesame oil. Deglaze with rice wine and reduce until pan is almost dry. Add the crab stock and bring to a simmer.

Whisk in the soy sauce, fish sauce, hoisin, oyster sauce, and Szechuan peppercorns. Allow the sauce to reduce by a quarter in volume. Add a couple of tbsp. water to the cornstarch to make a slurry. Slightly thicken the sauce with the slurry, and remove from heat. Toast the cracked black pepper over medium heat, and add to the sauce.

While the sauce is still warm, toss the crab fingers in a medium bowl with the rice flour, being sure to evenly coat the fingers with the flour. Fry the fingers in the vegetable oil at 350 degrees for about 2 minutes or until crispy. Remove the fingers from the oil and drain on paper towels.

Place the fingers in a medium bowl, and coat with sauce. Divide the rice among 6 small bowls. Divide the crab fingers evenly and place on top of the rice. Spoon extra sauce over the fingers and rice. Serves 6.

# Pork Belly *Bánh Mì*
### *Paul Artigues, Green Goddess*

2-3 slices cured and braised pork belly, ⅛-¼ in. thick
4-5 peeled, deveined shrimp (25-30-count size)
1 squirt Thai chili sauce
Foie gras butter
1 Dong Phuong roll, split most of the way through and toasted
8-12 thin slices English cucumber

Arugula
3 large basil leaves
Shredded carrots
Sliced pickled turnips
4 thin jalapeño slices, cut on diagonal
Fried shallots
Sliced green onions

Sear pork belly and remove from pan. Cook shrimp in same pan, in rendered pork fat, and add Thai chili sauce.

Spread foie gras butter on roll. Dress roll with cucumbers, arugula, basil, shredded carrots, pickled turnips, and jalapeño slices (with seeds). Add the pork belly, top with shrimp, and pour the rendered pork fat mixed with chili sauce over the sandwich. Garnish with shallots and green onions. Serves 1.

*Chef Paul Artigues of Green Goddess says that his pork belly* bánh mì *is a bestseller.* (Photograph by Lenny Delbert, Sr.)

# Shrimp Toast Sticks

*John Besh*

2 lb. raw shrimp
2 tbsp. chopped garlic
2 tbsp. chopped fresh ginger
1 cup chopped green onions
2 tbsp. sambal chili paste
¼ cup heavy cream

Salt to taste
1 pack feuille de brick dough
   (eggroll or spring-roll wrappers
   can be substituted)
2 cups canola oil

Place shrimp, garlic, ginger, onions, and sambal in a food processor. Begin pureeing, and add cream to smooth out the mixture. Season with salt to taste.

Cut brick dough sheets in fourths, and spread 1 heaping tsp. shrimp puree onto 1 sheet. Roll into a cylinder and set aside. Repeat with remaining sheets and filling. If you are not going to fry them right away, store in cornstarch to preventing from sticking.

In a large skillet over medium high, heat the oil and fry shrimp sticks in batches until golden brown and crispy. Makes 40 toast sticks with brick dough or 20 with eggroll wrappers.

# Meat Candy

*John Besh*

1 cup cornstarch
1 cup rice flour
2 cups hoisin sauce
½ cup sambal chili paste
½ cup rice vinegar

¼ cup honey
¼ cup chopped cilantro
1 lb. shaved beef short-rib meat
2 cups canola oil
8 leaves Bibb lettuce

In a small bowl, combine cornstarch and rice flour. Set aside.

In a medium bowl, combine hoisin, sambal, vinegar, honey, and cilantro. Marinate beef slices in ¼ cup of the hoisin mixture and set aside.

Dredge beef in cornstarch/rice-flour mix. In a large skillet over medium high, heat oil and fry beef in batches. Remove from pan to paper-towel-lined plate.

Once all batches have been fried, toss beef in remaining hoisin mixture and serve in lettuce cups. Serves 8.

## Bayou *Bánh Mì*

### *Andrew Gomila, Geaux Plates*

2 lb. boneless, skinless chicken thighs
6 cloves garlic, minced
4 stalks lemongrass, woody ends removed, finely chopped
½ cup fish sauce
½ tsp. dried chili flakes

1 tsp. sugar
Juice of 2 limes
2 lb. boudin (store bought or homemade)
6 *bánh mì* rolls or 8-in. French baguettes
½ stick butter, melted (optional)

Place chicken thighs in a zip-top bag. Combine garlic, lemongrass, fish sauce, chili flakes, sugar, and lime juice and pour over chicken thighs. Massage bag to coat thighs with marinade.

Allow to marinate for 1 hour on counter or overnight in refrigerator, up to 24 hours. Remove chicken thighs from marinade and place on a hot, preheated grill. Cook, turning once, 10-12 minutes or until juices run clear when thighs are pierced. Slice the chicken meat.

Prick boudin with a fork, and heat in microwave until hot all the way through. Alternatively, heat in a pot of gently simmering water. When hot, remove sausage from casings.

Split rolls, spread with butter if desired, and place cut side down on grill until lightly toasted, if desired.

*Gomila's bayou* bánh mì *is a Vietnamese dish with a New Orleans twist.* (Photograph by Lenny Delbert, Sr.)

## Garlic-Chili Aioli

3 egg yolks
¼ cup sriracha sauce
¼ cup Vietnamese garlic-chili paste
1-2 tsp. cayenne (optional)
6 cloves garlic, minced

1 tsp. Dijon mustard
Juice of 1 lime
½ tsp. salt
1 qt. vegetable oil

Combine all ingredients except oil in the bowl of a standing mixer fitted with the beater attachment. With mixer on high, slowly drizzle in oil until thick.

## Garnishes

Pickled carrots (store bought or homemade)
4-5 jalapeños, thinly sliced

1 bunch cilantro, stems removed, roughly chopped

To assemble the *bánh mì*, spread some aioli on top and bottom of each roll. Evenly divide boudin among rolls and spread along the bottoms like a paste. Evenly divide chicken slices among rolls. Top with carrots, jalapeños, and cilantro as desired. Serves 6.

# Steamed Wasabi Mussels

*Minh Bui, Café Minh*

1 tbsp. canola oil
1 tbsp. diced onion
1 lb. mussels (beards removed)
½ tsp. chopped garlic
2 oz. white wine

1 tbsp. wasabi (powder mixed with
   water to yield 1 tbsp.)
1 tsp. butter (optional)
Pinch dried chili pepper (optional)
Salt and pepper to taste

Heat a sauté pot with a cover until hot. Add oil, onion, mussels, and garlic. Stir.

Add wine and wasabi. Cover and let steam for 1 minute. Add butter if desired, adjust seasoning, and stir mussels until they open. Discard any unopened mussels.

# Shrimp Mirliton

*Minh Bui, Café Minh*

1 tsp. canola oil
1 tbsp. julienned onion
1 tsp. chopped garlic
24 peeled, tail-on shrimp, large or medium
2 tbsp. diced tomatoes

½ tsp. dried chili flakes
1 tbsp. tomato sauce
2 mirlitons, peeled and julienned
1 ladle chicken stock or water
Salt and pepper to taste

Heat oil in a pot until hot. Add onion, garlic, and shrimp, and sauté for 30 seconds—until the shrimp turn pink. Add tomatoes, dried chili, tomato sauce, mirliton, and chicken stock. Cover for 2 minutes.

Adjust seasoning with salt and pepper. Turn off heat and stir shrimp. Keep warm by placing a lid on the pot, until ready to served.

# Vietnamese-Style Chicken Wings
### *Emeril Lagasse*

3 to 3½ lb. chicken wings, separated at the joints, tips reserved for another use
½ cup roughly chopped lemongrass bases
¼ cup chopped shallots
¼ cup chopped fresh ginger
3 tbsp. chopped green onions (white part only)

3 tbsp. packed light brown sugar
2 tbsp. roughly chopped garlic
⅓ cup Vietnamese fish sauce
3 tbsp. freshly squeezed lime juice
3 tbsp. peanut oil
1 tsp. salt
¼ cup chopped dry-roasted salted peanuts
¼ cup chopped fresh cilantro

Rinse the wing pieces under cold running water and pat them dry with paper towels. Set them aside in a resealable plastic bag.

Combine the lemongrass, shallots, ginger, green onions, brown sugar, garlic, fish sauce, lime juice, and peanut oil in a food processor and process until smooth. Pour the marinade over the chicken wings, and seal the bag. Refrigerate overnight.

Preheat a grill to medium.

Remove the chicken wings from the marinade, reserving the marinade. Place the wings on the grill and season them with the salt. Cook, turning frequently and basting often with the marinade, for 15 minutes. Discard any remaining marinade and continue to grill the wings until cooked through, 8 to 10 minutes longer.

Place the chicken on a platter, and garnish with the chopped peanuts and cilantro. Serve immediately. Makes 4 to 6 appetizer servings.

*Recipe from* Emeril at the Grill, *HarperCollins Publishers, New York, 2009, courtesy MSLO, Inc. All rights reserved.*

*Chef Emeril Lagasse's Vietnamese-Style Chicken Wings are perfect for sharing among friends.* (Photograph by Lenny Delbert, Sr.)

# Beef Brisket *Phở*

*Emeril Lagasse*

4 lb. beef shank soup bones, beef knuckle bones, or combination
5½ qt. water
Two 3-in. cinnamon sticks
2 small dried chiles
1 tbsp. coriander seeds
1 tbsp. fennel seeds
8 whole star anise
4 cardamom pods
12 whole cloves
2 to 2½ lb. beef brisket
2 tbsp. kosher salt
1 to 2 tbsp. peanut oil
One 4-in. piece fresh ginger, cut crosswise into ¼-in.-thick slices
1 onion, unpeeled, halved
1 head garlic, halved crosswise
1 carrot, cut into 3 pieces

¼ cup fish sauce, plus more for serving
1½ tbsp. sugar
1½ tsp. salt
14 oz. rice stick noodles
Lime wedges, for serving
1 bunch fresh cilantro sprigs, for serving
1 bunch fresh mint sprigs, for serving
1 bunch fresh basil sprigs, preferably Thai basil, for serving
Bean sprouts, for serving
Romaine lettuce leaves, for serving
Sliced jalapeños, for serving
Thinly sliced onion, for serving
Sriracha sauce, for serving
Hoisin sauce, for serving

Add the beef bones to a large stockpot and cover with 12 cups of the water. Bring the water to a boil over high heat, reduce the heat to a simmer, and cook for 10 minutes. Using a ladle or large spoon, skim the foam that rises to the top and discard. Remove the bones, rinse them in cool water, and add them to the crock of a 6-qt. slow cooker. Discard the broth.

Combine the cinnamon sticks, dried chiles, coriander seeds, fennel seeds, star anise, cardamom pods, and cloves in a small bowl and set aside.

Season the brisket all over with the kosher salt. In a 12-in. skillet, heat 1 tbsp. oil over medium-high heat. Add the brisket, fat side down first, and brown for 3 to 4 minutes per side. Transfer the brisket to the slow cooker, fat side up.

Add ginger, onion, garlic, and carrot to the pan and brown for 1 minute (adding the remaining 1 tbsp. oil if necessary). Add the seasoning mix to the pan and toast for 1 minute. Transfer the contents of the skillet to the slow cooker and add the fish sauce, sugar, 1½ tsp. salt, and the remaining 10 cups water. Cook on high, undisturbed, for 6 hours.

Cook the rice stick noodles according to the package directions and set aside. Arrange the lime wedges, cilantro, mint, basil, bean sprouts, romaine, jalapeños, and sliced onion on a serving platter.

Remove the meat from the slow cooker and set aside on a cutting board. Strain the broth through a fine-mesh sieve into a small pot and cover to keep warm. Discard the vegetables and spices. Chop the meat from the soup bones and knuckle bones and set aside. Slice the brisket.

To serve, divide the noodles and meat among bowls. Ladle the hot broth over all and serve immediately. Each person should garnish the soup to taste with the ingredients on the serving platter and the condiments. Serves 4 to 6.

*Recipe from* Sizzling Skillets and Other One Pot Wonders, *HarperCollins Publishers, New York, 2011, courtesy MSLO, Inc. All rights reserved.*

## *Gỏi Ga Tom* (Shredded Chicken or Shrimp Salad)
### *Pho Tau Bay*

*Fish Sauce*

½ cup water
⅛ cup fish sauce

1 tbsp. vinegar
2 tbsp. sugar

Mix all ingredients thoroughly. Add lime juice and chilis to taste, if desired.

*Salad*

1 large head green cabbage, thinly sliced
1 large boiled boneless, skinless chicken breast, shredded, or 1½ lb. boiled shrimp, cut in half
½ yellow onion, thinly sliced
½ cup cilantro leaves

¼ cup *rau ram* leaves (Vietnamese cilantro)
⅓ cup sweet pickled carrots
½ oz. sesame oil
4 oz. crushed roasted peanuts
4 oz. fried shallots
1 sprig cilantro

Place cabbage, chicken or shrimp, onion, cilantro leaves, and carrots in a large mixing bowl, and toss together. Add oil and fish sauce, and distribute evenly. Top with peanuts, shallots, and sprig of cilantro. Serves 3-4.

Gỏi ga tom *from Pho Tau Bay* (Photograph courtesy Karl Takacs, Jr., of Pho Tau Bay)

# Shrimp Caminada Po' Boy

*Mark Falgoust, Grand Isle Restaurant*

## Compound Butter

1 lb. unsalted butter, softened
1 bunch cilantro, stems removed,
    chopped
Zest and juice of 3 limes
3 tbsp. Wang® chili powder

4 tbsp. sriracha sauce
2 tbsp. garlic-chili paste
1½ tbsp. salt
1 tsp. black pepper

Mix all ingredients very well until evenly distributed.

## Po' Boys

3 lb. peeled, deveined white
    shrimp (41/50 count size)
1 loaf French bread, cut into
    five 8-in. sections and split
    horizontally

Before cooking the shrimp, have the slaw and garnishes ready (see below).

In a cold, large sauté pan, add compound butter and shrimp at the same time over medium heat. Allow the butter to melt and slowly poach the shrimp so that they absorb the seasonings from a raw state. Stir until fully cooked. Add a generous amount of the shrimp and butter mixture to the bottom of each po'-boy section.

## Asian Slaw

| | |
|---|---|
| ½ head green cabbage, shredded | 2 tbsp. Wang® chili powder |
| ½ head Napa cabbage, shredded | 2 tbsp. salt |
| 1 red bell pepper, julienned | 1 tsp. black pepper |
| 1 large carrot, peeled and julienned | 3 tbsp. sugar |
| 1 cup rice wine vinegar | 1 tbsp. sriracha sauce |

Mix all slaw ingredients very well. Top shrimp in each po'-boy section with slaw mixture.

## Garnishes

| | |
|---|---|
| ½ cup fresh cilantro, stems removed | ½ cup fresh dill, stems removed |
| ½ cup fresh whole parsley leaves (Italian flat leaf) | ½ cup fresh basil, stems removed |

Divide the herbs among the po'-boy sections and place on top of the slaw. Top sections with top portions of bread. Serve with fries, potato salad, or chips. Makes 5 po' boys.

# Viet Dog

*Hoof & Cleaver*

⅓ cup soy sauce

2 tbsp. fish sauce

1 bunch green onions, finely
chopped

2 tsp. onion powder

2 tsp. garlic powder

1 tsp. ground black pepper

3 tbsp. honey

4 tbsp. sesame oil

5 tbsp. oyster sauce

12 lb. pork shoulder

Combine all ingredients except the pork and stir until very well combined. Make sure no clumps from the dry spices remain.

Cut the pork shoulder down into twelve 1-lb. pieces and submerge in the marinade overnight, in the refrigerator. Remove pork from the marinade after at least 12 hours, reserve the marinade, and grind all the pork through a small die on a meat grinder. Place pork back in the refrigerator after grinding.

While pork is chilling, take the remaining marinade and place in a blender or food processor with 1 cup ice. Blend until it is combined into a well-mixed slush.

Separate the pork into 4 equal portions. Working with a single portion at a time, place the pork in a food processor and begin processing. As the pork begins to break down, slowly add ¼ of the slush mix, until the pork has emulsified all the fat and slush mixture into a consistent emulsion.

Place each batch back into the refrigerator while working through the rest of the meat. When all the batches have been completed, let rest in the refrigerator for roughly 1 hour. While meat is chilling, prepare the sausage stuffer and soak sheep casings in water to remove the salt.

Stuff the sausage into the casings, working very slowly to make sure the meat fills the casing completely without leaving any air gaps. Link the sausage by rotating every other sausage in the opposite direction as the last. Grill and serve on a Dong Phuong steamed bun with fresh cilantro, jalapeño, cucumber, and pickled carrots.

# Beef *Phở*

*Doson's Noodle House*

3 lb. beef bone
1½ lb. flank steak
6 gal. water
¼ oz. star anise
¼ oz. cinnamon sticks
Cloves

1 large onion, baked
3-in. piece ginger, sliced
1 tbsp. salt
1 tbsp. sugar
Rice vermicelli

Add beef bones and beef to a pot of water. Put seasonings, except salt and sugar, in a cloth bag and place in water. Bring pot to a boil.

Lower heat and let pot of water simmer for 6 hours. During the first hour, remove the cooked steak. Once the meat is cooled, cut it into thin slices and set aside.

After 6 hours, remove the beef bones and bag. Strain; 2½ gal. stock should remain. Add salt and sugar to the stock.

Dip noodles in boiling water for 2 seconds. Place in a bowl. Top noodles with sliced beef.

Pour beef stock into the bowl. Top, according to preference, with basil, cilantro, lime, bean sprouts, sriracha sauce, and hoisin sauce. Serves 6.

# Acknowledgments

This book is based on the film *Vietnamese Cuisine in New Orleans*, which debuted on WYES-TV in October 2012. While producing this film, I collaborated with Lenny Delbert, Sr., and Peggy Scott Laborde. Thanks to Lenny Delbert, Sr., the talented videographer behind the film and the book, for his time, encouragement, and humor. Thanks to Peggy Scott Laborde, the accomplished documentary filmmaker and author, whose work inspired me to pursue a career in broadcast journalism. I am honored that she narrated my film and thankful for her feedback and support. Also, thanks to Beth Arroyo Utterback and the other excellent staff members at WYES-TV.

Most of the people included in this book were also in the film. I'm grateful for their expertise and enthusiasm on this subject. Thanks to Chef John Besh for participating in my first filmed interview and introducing me to his team and Fr. Vien Nguyen. Very special thanks to the local Vietnamese, especially Hanh and Vinh Tran, who shared their personal stories with me. I am humbled by their resilience and love for life.

Thanks to the incredible staff at Pelican Publishing, including Kathleen Calhoun Nettleton, Nina Kooij, Antoinette de Alteriis, Scott Campbell, Terry Callaway, and my dear friend Michelle Lesslie. I have enjoyed working with them over the years. And they continue to publish beautiful books about the culture and history of the city that I am so proud to call home—New Orleans. Thanks to my mentor and friend, Romney Richard, and to my creative, supportive colleagues in the publishing and film world.

From the Jumonvilles to the Pfefferles, I am blessed to have such a wonderful family.

Thanks to my grandparents, cousins, aunts, uncles, and Fr. Bob Massett—he gave me my first computer so that I could begin my writing career. Thanks to my three older brothers—Keith, Erik, and Karl, Jr.—who have a strong work ethic and reverence for family. They are always rooting for me. Thanks to Heather, Lindsay, Brittany (my traveling buddy throughout Vietnam), and Jose David. Finally, I must extend a heartfelt thank-you to my mother, Jeanne, and father, Karl. I am eternally grateful for their love and support. At an early age, I announced that one day I'll travel and write books. They have since encouraged me to pursue my dreams and smile along the way.

I aim to live a life that makes them proud.

# Glossary

*aquaponics.* A sustainable food-production system that combines traditional aquaculture—raising aquatic animals, such as koi fish—with hydroponics. Hydroponics allows the cultivation of plants in water, in a symbiotic environment.

*bánh bao.* Steamed dumplings with meat fillings, such as minced barbecue pork.

*bánh chưng.* A sweet rice cake shaped as a square and sometimes filled with mung-bean paste or barbecue pork. It is traditionally served during Tết.

*bánh chuoi nep.* Steamed banana with sticky rice.

*bánh cuốn.* A rice batter that is steamed, filled with a small portion of meat, and rolled into a dumpling.

*bánh mì.* Airy baguette bread made with or including rice flour. The *bánh mì* sandwich contains Vietnamese mayonnaise or pâté, charcuterie, herbs, and pickled vegetables.

*bánh phở.* The long, flat rice noodles used in *phở*.

*bánh tráng.* The translucent rice paper used in summer rolls and other Vietnamese appetizers.

*bánh xèo.* Also known as a Vietnamese crepe. This is prepared by pouring rice batter with turmeric onto a hot, well-oiled skillet. The cook then tosses slivers of pork loin or pork belly, shrimp, onion, and bean sprouts onto the sizzling cake. Once the crepe is cooked, it is folded into the shape of an omelet.

*bap chè.* Sweet corn dessert cup.

*bo kho.* A stew containing slow-cooked beef, broth, vegetables, and herbs.

*boba tea.* A sweet beverage, also known as bubble tea, that contains tea, fruit, and tapioca balls.

*boudin.* A type of sausage created in Louisiana.

*bún.* Commonly referred to as rice vermicelli, which are made from rice flour.

*cà phê sữa đá.* Also known as Vietnamese iced coffee. This beverage contains strong coffee, slowly dripped over a glass of ice. Sometimes a generous portion of condensed milk sits at the bottom of the glass.

*cám ơn.* The Vietnamese way of saying "thank you."

*daikon.* A white radish with a mild flavor, cultivated in parts of Asia. In Vietnamese cuisine, it is pickled and placed on *bánh mì* sandwiches.

*gỏi cuốn.* Moist rice paper wrapped around slivers of pork or prawns, savory greens, and rice vermicelli (*bún*). *Gỏi cuốn* is also known as a "summer roll."

*hoisin sauce.* A dipping sauce with a slightly sweet flavor, made from such ingredients as soybeans, sesame seed, garlic, and sweet potato.

*mung bean sprouts.* Used as a garnish for *phở* or *gỏi cuốn*. Crispy bean sprouts have a mild, earthy flavor.

*nước mắm.* A fish sauce prepared by marinating raw, salt-cured anchovies in a barrel. The liquid is then extracted.

*phở.* A soup made of flavorful beef or chicken broth, long rice noodles, and a type of meat. It's often topped with herbs and sauces.

*po'-boy sandwich.* A popular New Orleans sandwich, consisting of meat or seafood and various dressings on French bread.

*sâm bổ lượng.* A sweet drink that contains Job's tears, dried longans, red jujubes, lotus seeds, thinly sliced seaweed, strips of ginger, ginkgo nuts, water, sugar, and crushed ice.

*soda chan.* A refreshing beverage made of lime juice, soda water, and sugar, poured over a glass of ice.

*star anise.* A star-shaped spice that has a flavor similar to licorice.

*Tết.* The Vietnamese lunar new year. This annual celebration begins on the first day of the first month of the lunar calendar, which is usually late January or early February, and ends on the third day.

*thit nuong.* Barbecue pork.

**Vietnamese mayonnaise.** Typically contains slowly blended egg yolks, an acid, salt, and oil.

# Index